THE
WOMAN
OF
WYRRD

The Arousal of the Inner Fire

LYNN V. ANDREWS

HarperSanFrancisco
A Division of HarperCollins*Publishers*

. . .

FIRST EDITION

Text design by Irene Imfeld
Composition by Wilsted & Taylor

Library of Congress Cataloging-in-Publication Data

Andrews, Lynn V.
      The woman of Wyrrd : the arousal of the inner fire / Lynn V. Andrews. — 1st ed.
            p.   cm.
      ISBN 0–06–250066–X (alk. paper) :
      1. Women — Religious life.   2. Andrews, Lynn V.   3. New Age movement.   I. Title.
BL625.7.A54   1990
299'.93 — dc20   89–46455
                                                                                CIP

90   91   92   93   94   RRD(H)   10   9   8   7   6   5   4   3   2   1

. . .

For my mother,
Rosalyn Staples,
who is teaching
me to remember

. . .

*Breaking the silence
that turns around
the double edge of seeing.
I have called you
into the night moon
because we have come
to learn the end of waiting.*

CONTENTS

. . .

This is a true story.
Some of the names and the places in this
book have been changed to protect the
privacy of those involved.

. . .

PREFACE

HAVE YOU EVER WONDERED what you are doing on this earth, why you are alive, and what meaning there is to the pain that we all experience?

When I was in Nepal and Tibet in the spring of 1988, I asked these questions of my teacher, Agnes Whistling Elk. We were sitting on top of a mountain in the foothills of the Annapurna Himal. Agnes chuckled a little at my questions. She pointed her knobby brown finger at the face of Annapurna, whose crown was obscured by fluffy white clouds.

"We're like that mountain," she said. "The extent of her power and beauty is hidden from view; at the top she is lost in a dream. Before we are born onto this earth walk, we wait for a great blessing — our chance to be born onto earth. We know that we come here to be enlightened. When we are born, the dream begins. Like the cloud hiding the mountaintop, the dream obscures our true vision. We must gather a strong wind to blow away the clouds. Then we can see, truly see, the whole of our being — the silent mountain that we are. That is what life is all about: waking up from the dream. We have come here to become enlightened, yet it is the one thing that we are most afraid of.

"To be initiated is to have the veils of ignorance torn away. That is what our work together is about. For you to be initiated into our circle, the Sisterhood of the Shields, one of our members must first pass on to the other side. There was a great woman, the old, wise one among us, who held great power and had memorized all the old ways. She chose her death so that you could become initiated. Old Annapurna is not unlike our friend and sister who made this choice. She was magnificent in her white shields of serenity. She taught me about the balance of vulnerability and power one needs to become an enlightened being. She was a confuser of the clouds and could move through the air like a beam of light. She was our prime mover for a long time."

"What was her name?" I asked.

"She has asked to reveal her name and her teachings to you herself," Agnes said, watching me with her head cocked to one side like a crow.

"But how can that be?" I asked.

· ix ·

"On our journey into Tibet, if you pass the initiation, you will be able to answer your own question," Agnes said, getting up from the flat brown stone we had been sitting on.

No amount of questioning got me an answer. I had to find it myself. When I found the Valley of Luktang in Tibet, I discovered a place of dreaming where information is exchanged in very unusual ways — ways that I had experienced before particularly in Australia in what is called the Sacred Dreamtime. It was made clear to me that this extraordinary woman would teach me about a life that we had shared together a long time ago. Through the experience of this life together, she would instruct me again, as she once had as my teacher. Very few of the details were given to me as yet, but I understood that we were part of an ancient and powerful magic, the way of Wyrrd, whose great secrets far exceed what we know now. These secrets have been preserved down through civilization; they have been disguised and hidden in the mountains, in rocks, in the sky, in the sacred waters of the earth. I was told that when the time was right, certain people would be chosen to recover these ancient teachings and bring them to light. My teacher in that life of so long ago would be my guide in the way of Wyrrd; my next journey would be with this wise old woman. As Grandmother, she would help me to understand, through our experiences together, how each of us carries a spirit shield that can be imprinted with knowledge from one lifetime to another.

. . .

In writing about my experiences with the Woman of Wyrrd, I was again faced with a problem of language and translation that I have always struggled with in my books. Many books have been artfully written using the English of long ago throughout. However, I came to a decision with the Sisterhood that because the aspects of Wyrrd (the study of power and magic in ancient Europe) that I was attempting to explain were already so remote and unusual, I should use language as clear and familiar as possible. There are times when that decision may diminish the reader's experience of ancient England. But this is a book of magical teachings, not an anthropological study, though I would have been very proud to have discovered a way to express the lush intricacies of those ancient words and terms with the subtlety of the powers of Wyrrd that Grandmother imparted to me.

IN SPIRIT, RESPECT, AND LOVE FOR THE WOMAN OF WYRRD,
LYNN ANDREWS

CHAPTER · 1

FINDING
A
DISTANT
REALITY

Look for nothing
to take us out of here.
Ramshackle.
A word that divinely
chains us to earth.

Ramshackle wind
ramshackle fire
ramshackle house of our bodies

like a lizard
hiding under the blue tint
of English holly
as if the red berries
will sustain us
all the way home.

T HERE IS A SECRET core in all of us," Agnes Whistling Elk said as she watched me fidget under her steady gaze. She had instructed me to come and discuss the next phase of our journey together.

"Why do I feel this sense of longing — as if I were trying to find my way home?" I asked her.

Agnes, Ruby Plenty Chiefs, Ruby's apprentice July, a young Cree girl, and I were sitting around a simple wooden table in Agnes's one-room cabin in the far north of Manitoba, Canada. It was an early evening in spring, and the scent of young grass and pine was in the air. July stoked the fire in the old iron stove and brought each of us a cup of mint leaf tea as we talked.

"Your evolution as an apprentice is like giving birth to a child. The longing you feel is the longing every woman feels for the unborn, whether the unborn is a state of enlightenment, a life in the form of a baby, or a work of art," Agnes said, as she sipped her tea and sniffed the fragrant, minty steam rising from the liquid. Her long gray braids rested on her red-and-black Pendleton shirt.

"This experience, this far memory that is in you, my daughter, is more than longing. It is part of the core of your existence as a human being," Agnes said. "It is different from your other journeys; its source is in another hoop of existence, from your past. It comes from what you might call your spirit history. But you will come to know of its form in the future."

"I don't fully understand what you mean. But I do know that something has been changing me, even before it has taken form as a reality in my mind," I said.

"This spirit birth will change you forever," Agnes said.

Ruby pinched my arm and giggled. "Lynn, you should be used to changes by now. You've changed a lot since we met you, thank the Great Spirit for little favors," Ruby said. She cupped her knobby fingers over the imaginary "little favors" on the table and winked at me. An eerie silvery light reflected off her blind eyes, making me fidget even more.

"Thanks, Ruby, you're always a big help," I said as everyone laughed at my discomfort. Finally, I laughed too, as Crow, with perfect timing, hopped onto the windowsill above the sink and pecked rhythmically on the window, seeming to applaud Ruby's teasing. Agnes tilted her head from side to side, imitating Crow. This was a game they often played. Crow would finally ruffle his wings, hop up and down, and caw madly to be let in for a morsel of food. This time July opened the window and offered the huge bird some crusts of bread Agnes had been saving for him.

Crow cawed loudly in Agnes's direction and flew off with his prize gripped firmly in his beak.

Agnes continued, "When we were in Nepal last year, I told you something very important. I told you that a great sister of ours had chosen her death so that you could be initiated into the Sisterhood of the Shields."

"I remember I asked about this woman, what her name was, and why she had done such a thing. And you left me hanging," I said a little impatiently.

"Not exactly hanging," Ruby said, smiling to herself, "but now that you mention it . . ."

"I told you that our sister, the woman who had been our great prime mover for a very long time, wanted to tell you herself," Agnes said, ignoring Ruby.

"How is that possible, Agnes?"

"She will come to you in the Dreamtime," Agnes answered.

"But when? Before I arrived here, in my dreaming in Los Angeles, I felt as if she were often knocking on some invisible door inside me, as if the veils of consciousness would not part and let me see her. I'm so frustrated."

Agnes looked at me a long time. She turned her head a little sideways and scanned me mostly through her left eye. Finally she heaved a big sigh. "You are too much of the world," she said. "Your teaching work in Los Angeles and New Mexico has brought you too much into contact with other people."

"But you're the one who said, 'You must live in the big cities of the world. Where do you think healing is needed? Certainly not here in the wilderness. You must let the eagles fly, and take what you have learned about the ancient way of woman, and teach your people.' You put me into the world, Agnes. All I wanted to do was stay here with you," I said. Tears of frustration welled up in my eyes.

"It is true, Little Wolf. We have given you quite a difficult task." Agnes laid her hand over mine. "Its difficulty is why we in the Sisterhood must remain so hidden and secret. To be able to dream, to work on other levels daily, to help balance the energies of Mother Earth, we must never leave our center." Agnes patted the area over her navel. "It requires an extraordinary effort to maintain this shaman stance. If any of us got involved in politics, in public discussions, in the everyday needs of human personality, we could never sustain the power and centeredness we need to continue our work. To be known would be to lose our power. That is the truth of it. Higher wisdom has always been held in secret to protect it for those who are prepared for it. When light shines, the darkness encroaches on the edges of brilliance to define it and give the light an even truer definition," Agnes said.

"Then she will really come?"

"Oh, yes, but because of the intensity of your life, we will need to help you a little," Agnes said, running her long, dark fingers over a red-tailed hawk feather that lay on the table.

"How do you mean?" Her tone made me nervous.

"Because we have asked so much of you in the world, we are going to help you relax so you can dream more easily," Agnes said, touching my shoulder.

"She means you're a nervous wreck," Ruby leaned over and hissed in my ear.

"You're probably right, Ruby, but you don't have to be mean," I said, teasing her by pretending to be annoyed.

"We will build you a special lodge just for your dreaming," Agnes told me, ignoring Ruby again.

"Isn't there a Dreamlodge used in traditional Indian ceremonies?" I asked.

"Sometimes, but this one will be different, and its energy will be different. This Dreamlodge will be for you to dream in, and just for you and this specific purpose. It will help you to remember your spirit history," Agnes said.

"You have told me before to leave the past behind and not dwell on it, to eradicate any thoughts about my history. Why, now, are you asking me to do this?"

"This is not your history in this lifetime or even in recent lifetimes, my daughter. This has to do with the ancient teachings that you are learning now. It is important to see the many faces of your God. The Great Spirit has manifested light on Mother Earth in many ways and at many times throughout history. It is important for you to experience the depth of what that means. There is a key to all that I say to you. Perhaps you will discover that key." Agnes drained her teacup and abruptly got up and left the cabin.

I got up to follow her, but Ruby grabbed my arm and pulled me down. A gust of cold night air filled the cabin as the old plank door scraped across the floor and shut noisily.

"What are you doing?" I asked Ruby, who still held my sleeve in her fist. I wanted to catch up with Agnes and continue our conversation.

"Impatience, Little Wolf—when will you learn?"

"But I want to ask Agnes something."

"You're too far away," Ruby said, shaking her head. Her long gray braids brushed back and forth over her navy blue shawl.

"Well, I can't get my chair any closer to you, Ruby!"

"I don't mean your chair. You are far away from this moment we are sharing."

I stared at her. The light from the gas lantern flickered across the deep creases in her dark brown skin. Her opaque eyes narrowed as she explored a world unknown to me and my normal vision.

"I'm sorry, Ruby. I didn't know that you wanted to speak to me."

"What you are looking for is all around you in this room," Ruby said, making an expansive gesture with her right arm taking in the entire interior of the cabin.

I looked around us and shrugged my shoulders. "I don't understand, and besides I didn't know I was looking for anything."

"Oh, really. I suppose you've been coming here all these years just for fun."

"I didn't realize you meant *that*."

"What's 'that'?" Ruby asked.

"Well, truth, I guess."

"Truth, you guess! Well, that's not bad for starters, I suppose. Truth is everywhere around you. It cannot leave your presence, but you can choose to leave truth."

"How can both be true?"

"It's a matter of awareness, isn't it?" Ruby asked.

"You mean, you can choose not to be aware?"

"Yes, your next exploration is a journey of the soul. You could miss everything by stepping out of your essential awareness into fear and confusion," Ruby said, tapping her fingers softly on the table.

"But how can I help being afraid sometimes?"

"You can live more fully in your heart. Love is the bridge you have built with faith. Now you must have the trust to walk across the abyss of a vast darkness. That bridge is love, and it forms the connection between your body and your spirit," Ruby said, letting go of my sleeve.

"What can I do? I still feel helpless," I said as I sat down again.

"That is good." Ruby smiled at me.

"Why is it good to feel helpless?"

"Because when you journey out of the ego lodge, you drop away from your worn, everyday path into a helpless state; you become humble. You look around with frightened eyes, and you pray to the Great Spirit. That is a beginning. In your prayer you will find beauty."

"Ruby, what does beauty have to do with humility?" I asked.

"They both throw you back onto yourself. Everything you experience on this earth walk is part of a great mirror. Every experience makes you see yourself in a different way. Humbleness is just another mirror. Like beauty, it is an experience that puts you in touch with the Great Spirit. When you are humble you are no longer far away. You become present, and you do your ceremony or you pray to the Great Spirit for help."

Ruby pressed the back of my hand with her fingers. They felt calloused and strong. She faced me, raising her eyebrows, and said nothing more.

I started to speak, but I realized I had nothing else to say. She was right. I was feeling very humble and quiet inside. There was no more need to talk. July and Ruby put on their parkas, gave me a hug, and left the cabin very silently. As they were leaving, Agnes slipped in quietly and smiling, first at Ruby and July leaving and then at me. Everything seemed to be understood. We were all tired. It was time to offer our prayers and go to sleep.

· · ·

The next morning I could hardly wake up. I first awoke with the dawn, only to sense Agnes leaving the cabin. I couldn't seem to move. I thought I must be exhausted from traveling, and I fell back into a dreamless sleep. At eleven o'clock I woke again with a start. Agnes walked into the one room of the cabin, shuffling her feet noisily on the plank floor and bringing with her a smell of willow branches and spring sap.

"Little Wolf, all curled up, are you ready to see your Dreamlodge?" Agnes asked as she flung her parka over a nail on the wall and began setting out biscuits and tea.

"Sure," I said, excited but not awake enough to say much else.

"How are you feeling?" Agnes asked me as we sat across from each other over lunch. Warm beacons of sunlight shone through the windows and reflected off the bundles of herbs, the drums, feathers, and rattles hanging from the rafters.

"A little apprehensive," I replied.

Agnes raised her eyebrows at me and pursed her lips thoughtfully.

"We can't change this world through war," she said, spooning honey onto her biscuit. "It is time to celebrate and make our own ceremonies by dancing and singing and learning to live our dreams. But first we must know how to dream."

I nodded my head and sipped my tea.

"What is the first step to dreaming?" Agnes asked.

I thought back to our time in Australia with Genevee and the Sacred Dreamtime: "An ability to visualize."

"Visualization is essential, but what is behind being able to visualize?"

"Being able to believe in your imagination," I replied.

"That's right. But remember that believing is a tricky concept. A belief structure not only limits your imagining, but also limits your entire consciousness."

"Would a better word be *trusting?*" I asked.

"Yes, trusting what comes is part of loving. It is your trust that builds the bridge between this physical dream we live in and the dream of your spirit. In a sense that is what love is made of—the totality of mind and soul. The bridge or connection, then, is trust. When you found Wind-horse, your spirit-man, he came to you on a beam of trust. It was not your imagination that created him, but it was your imagination that found him and allowed him to ride across that beam of light into your heart. You never doubted his being, and so you never limited his existence."

I was silent for several moments, letting her words sink in. "I understand, Agnes, but what Ruby said last night was true."

"What did she say?"

"She talked to me about being far away and too much in the world."

"She's right," Agnes said, nodding her head, "but you have the ability to dream, and it will not take you long to come home."

"Are you sure?"

"Well, let's go down by the creek and see." Agnes grabbed her shawl and threw me my parka.

We walked down the winding path through the poplars to the mossy creek banks. The sunlight was warm, but there was still an undercurrent of cool northern air that made me thankful for my parka. We found the two flat teaching rocks that we have been sitting on for so many years. I touched the gray, smooth stone lovingly with my fingers and stroked the dead leaves and sand off her surface. I sat down next to Agnes.

For several minutes we sat quietly just relaxing and watching the narrow stream in front of us. Dead Man's Creek, full this time of year, rushed by us. The sunlight reflected in rainbow prisms off the water, as if quartz crystals were imbedded in the brown sand beneath the surface. The flow of water has always mesmerized me. I sat there, immediately transfixed by its movement, which contrasted with the stillness inside me.

"Let yourself float, Black Wolf. Let yourself float with the river," Agnes said as she began to sing softly in Cree.

A long time went by, and then Agnes began to speak. "The flow of the water empties me of myself. I sit here in spirit waiting for the world and my people to stop fighting. In anger and war there is only hardness. People and the world become solid, and they forget the river. They forget how to flow. To find the river of your spirit is to find freedom. There is no need to come up against anyone. When you become rigid in the world, then the world has no more need of you, and your spirit slowly drains away like blood spilled onto sand. Just float with the water, and let the Great Spirit flow with you," Agnes said.

"I feel an emptiness, Agnes, whenever I sit here by the creek."

"That emptiness is a prayer. You are making a place for the Great Spirit to live inside you."

"It's the movement of the water, isn't it, Agnes? It's the movement of the physical into spirit."

"If you need to explain this feeling, my daughter, perhaps it is best just to call it an opening that allows something still unknown to happen."

After several minutes had passed and I felt clear and relaxed, Agnes nodded her head toward a stand of willows upstream.

"Come, let's explore your Dreamlodge."

CHAPTER · 2

THE
SACRED
DREAMLODGE

WE FOLLOWED A DEER track along the creek. What I first noticed was what looked like deadfall in the forest. Then I realized it was the lodge. As I came closer to it, it was clear to me that the two old women had put a tremendous amount of work into this lodge, and I was very touched.

"Agnes, you have built me a most beautiful Dreamlodge. Thank you so much. I am full," I said, holding my hand over my heart.

Agnes looked at me with a twinkle in her eye. "I hope you will dream well, my daughter," she said.

I touched the bent willow saplings of the lodge and looked at the intricate weave they had created. It was quite a large structure. It stood taller than I am and was at least fifteen feet across. Agnes walked around to the east door and called for me to come join her. Beautiful river stones had been put around the perimeter, each one carefully chosen and carefully placed so that they all fit together like a stone wall.

I pulled aside the red-and-yellow Hudson Bay blanket that hung over the entrance, thrilled to discover the interior of my Dreamlodge for the first time. The inside of the lodge was covered with skins and Indian blankets. Most of the blankets looked Navajo, with their reds and blacks and whites and blues, beautiful old designs. On the floor were more blankets. In the center was a fire pit and in it a pile of wood was burning. The inside of the lodge was very warm. Sheepskins had been piled high at one end and a blanket sewn in the shape of a pillow so that I could lie down.

"I want you to be very comfortable and at ease here, so that you can completely forget your body when you are working," Agnes said. "We will keep the fire stoked so that you will not need to worry."

Continuing to look around, I noticed glints of light, prismatic colors reflecting off the floor of the lodge, and I noticed many crystals set around in special places. Then I saw an altar at one end of the lodge. In front of it were many of my sacred things—crystals, beaded bundles, and my personal pipe—on my unrolled medicine blanket. Prayer sticks, feathers, and my walking stick were placed alongside. My eyes were drawn to something hanging over the altar. It looked like a gold necklace with an amulet, medieval perhaps. Carved within the amulet was a symbol that I didn't know. I looked questioningly at Agnes.

"Go and examine that piece hanging over the altar. It is magical, and it has to do with your work in the Dreamtime to come," Agnes said.

I walked over to the altar, stepping carefully so as not to disturb the carefully arranged blankets. The symbol within the amulet was encased in a circle made of what looked like gold, shining a dull yellow in the firelight. Inside the circle was a symbol that looked like a Celtic cross with a diamond in the center that reflected my face like a tiny mirror. There were other runelike designs that I could not identify or interpret, but they seemed familiar in a way that brought tears to my eyes.

I continued to gaze at the design. I touched it, felt it, my fingers running over the smooth surface. The designs struck an ancient chord inside me, a memory chord, but I could not quite grasp its meaning. All I was sure of was how familiar it felt, that at some time I had worn this design, maybe even this exact necklace, around my neck.

"Agnes, I can feel the weight of it around my neck."

Agnes looked at me. She touched the edge of the circle on the design. "Yes, my daughter, it is possible that you wore this a long time ago."

I wondered if I should ask to put it on. Then I realized that it was somehow not yet appropriate, and at the same moment Agnes smiled to herself as if she understood what I was thinking.

"There will be time, my daughter. There will be much time. You will know what is right to do. Now, explore your Dreamlodge. I will leave you, and we will eat dinner together later," Agnes said. She left the lodge.

I walked around, slowly making myself familiar with every crevice, every blanket, every piece of fur from the animal kingdom — those sacred animals that had given away so that we might live. There was a small jaguar stool in front of the altar. I went over to it and sat down before my sacred things. I lit a candle that I found there. Then from it I lit a rope of sweet grass that began to smoke. Using an eagle feather, I spread the smoke and blessed my sacred things. Taking up sage and cedar, I also lit them. I smudged and cleared the interior of the Dreamlodge to the four directions and went outside and did the same.

Back inside the Dreamlodge, I left the sage and cedar burning in an abalone shell next to me as I sat down at my altar and prayed to the Great Spirit. I prayed to the Creator for help on my journey into the unknown, and I asked my guides and my allies for protection. I asked for power and vision, and asked my medicine, my wolf, and the other beings that protect me and guide me to help me on this walk into the Sacred Dream. I asked that they protect and guide me, guide my spirit footsteps, and help me to clear away the barriers to my spirit history. I asked the spirits to call me, to help me to let go of the physical problems of my life, to let go of the world, at least long enough to understand the truth and the teachings, so that I would be able to understand with my heart and my soul everything that this new teacher would impart to me.

I finished my prayers, and then I reached for the necklace and placed it around my neck. It felt heavy and oddly warm, as if it had just been worn. Suddenly I realized how sleepy I was. I went over to the sheepskins that had been laid out for me, and I lay down on them and went almost instantly to sleep. As I dozed off, I heard the voice of Agnes in my head.

"My daughter, the circle of truth that hangs around your neck, the ancient necklace — I want you to know that as a configuration of wisdom. Think of the four directions, the crosses that represent the four directions within the circle. See into your far memory. Think back to a time before you knew me, a time before you knew of America. Think back a long way. Breathe deeply, and completely relax your body. Think back a long way.

"See the tunnel. It is forming at the back of your mind, a tunnel of darkness that spirals down and down. Will your consciousness into that tunnel. Know that I will protect you. Move with trust and clarity, and know that no harm could possibly ever come to you in this lodge of your dreams. Let your consciousness wander, and explore the unlimited dimensions of your mind and your knowing. Look into your subconscious, and let it provide you with the trail that you need to follow. See the light, way, way down at the end of this spiraling, sacred tunnel, and move toward that light. Know that you will come to that light, and for a time your consciousness will encompass that light. You and your consciousness and that light will become one."

For a long while there was silence and then the sound of a high wind. I felt weightless.

"As you journey toward that light, see in front of your mind's eye the amulet that rests on your chest. Focus your attention on the center of the cross. That's right, my daughter. There is a mirrorlike diamond at the center. See the reflection of your own eye looking back at you, and look into that eye steadily and long."

She paused a moment and then went on.

"As you look into the eye, the eye of your own being, the eye of your ageless spirit, move your consciousness into the eye, right into the pupil. That's right, my daughter, you are beginning to see with the eye of the cross. Now look out into the world through that eye. What is it you see?"

Slowly, Agnes's voice began to fade, and I realized that I must have merged with the light I had seen in the distance, because no longer was I in the tunnel. I was looking out into a vast green countryside that was completely unknown to me. The trees looked like oaks, maybe king oaks and alders. There was unfamiliar underbrush with red berries and lots of clover. It was quite cool and damp, but as I looked down, I realized I was wearing a long dress, its bodice high and tight, and a flowing cape of velvet that was lined with a very warm material, like wool.

I was walking quickly down a path next to a river, a narrow river, and I was looking for someone. I obviously knew where I was going. I looked down at my hands; they were very young. There was a beautiful ring on my finger, a ruby. I looked down at it, caressing the smooth stone with my fingers. I looked ahead, pulled the hood of my cape over my hair, and moved on with a sense of urgency, as if I were late for a meeting with someone.

The rolling hills were covered with deep green grass, and the air smelled of damp earth. There were no houses in sight. It did not feel like the wilderness, but I felt though I was out in the countryside. I also felt strongly that someone was waiting for me. I could not imagine who. I had no idea where I was, but an instinct inside me told me where to go, so I followed it, as if it were the most natural thing to do. I wondered what country I was in. It felt familiar and yet very foreign to the rolling plains of Manitoba.

Out of the mist that lay over one area of the green meadow, I heard a startling sound. At first I stopped, not knowing what it was. Then I realized it was a woman's cry. I looked up toward the crest of the hill that loomed through the mist. Silhouetted against a low hanging sun stood a beautiful young woman, her auburn hair flowing back in the sunlight. She raised her hands to the sky as if she were praying to a sun god. She uttered another scream, sounding like a bird of prey.

A moment later a peregrine falcon with a huge wing span circled above her. He screamed a reply to her, and then, with his wings tucked, headed for her right arm, which was wound and tied in leather. As the falcon approached the woman, he put his talons out in front of him, flapped his wings, and landed gently on her arm. Woman and bird looked into each other's eyes. Very slowly she raised her other arm and caressed the top of the bird's head with a feather held in her hand. He softened and fluffed his wings and began to preen himself. The woman was very definitely his mistress. Never had I seen a falcon behave so obediently.

This mysterious woman had a loving, respectful relationship with the bird. I could tell that she had never abused the bird, nor had the bird ever attacked her. One could see by their air of mutual respect that there was no harm between them.

Still carrying the bird on her arm, the woman walked down the hill and disappeared into the forest.

· · ·

There was a crackling sound, and suddenly the image faded, and I was back in Manitoba lying in the Dreamlodge. Agnes and Ruby were smudging me with cedar smoke, and I lay there wide-eyed. The feeling of being the girl in the cape and seeing the woman with the falcon had been so strong that I was confused about where I really was.

"Agnes, I don't know if I can do this," I said. My body felt cold and stiff, as if my blood had stopped flowing. Agnes stroked my forehead with her eagle feather.

"That's what the woman was doing with her falcon!" I exclaimed, trying to sit up. Ruby pushed me back on my pillow and lifted the necklace from around my neck. Agnes took it from her and hung it back over the altar.

"Always replace the necklace when you are finished dreaming. It is a dream necklace and very sacred to the Sisterhood. While you wear it, your spirit will want to dreamwalk," Agnes told me. "Now, what woman? What falcon?" she asked. "Start at the beginning, and take your time."

I went back slowly into my mind and recalled my dreaming in words for her. The old woman nodded as I continued.

"But it hurts to come back into this body," I said, rubbing my legs. "And I wasn't gone very long."

"Oh?" Agnes said, looking up at the moon shining through the smoke hole in the roof of the lodge.

I was astounded that it was dark already. "How can that be? Hours must have passed. Does that mean that time takes longer in the dream?" I asked.

"It means that time is not the issue here. Time is irrelevant, shall we say."

Agnes and Ruby smiled knowingly at each other. I looked up into their faces, at that moment so familiar and yet so strange.

"I am much younger, perhaps only thirteen or fourteen, in this other life. How can that happen?" I asked.

"It doesn't matter. Your spirit has come of age even in that lifetime. You may seem physically younger, but your capacity to learn and grow is the same as an adult's. It often happens that way. But come now. Let's eat something, and then you must sleep," Agnes said, helping me up.

CHAPTER · 3

THE
LADY
IN THE
MIST

Whoever carries
the strong dreams
wakes up in a new world.
Here
the air is clear
like bright fire
surrounded by a darkness
that nourishes us.

THE NEXT DAY I SPENT resting, helping Agnes repair her smokehouse, which needed new hinges on the door, and getting to know my Dreamlodge even more intimately. The lodge was becoming precious to me, and I wanted to spend time blessing it and caring for its presence.

. . .

That night I entered into another spirit journey. This time I began to feel a rhythm to the sounds of nature that were foreign to me. I had a sense now of being an older girl, probably in Europe or England, I thought, because of the leafy green trees and green fields with low stone walls. It felt like centuries ago. I was a lonely girl named Catherine, of good blood, able to read and cipher, and with a great thirst for knowledge. I knew that the woman with the falcon I had seen before was important to me. There was a great mystery in my life, echoed by the mist that lay over the hills and forest groves. I felt slightly uneasy, but I knew more about myself this time and where I was going. I knew my family was connected to the royal court in some way and that I was much alone these days.

As I dreamed, I moved more deeply into a sense of the language I spoke as Catherine. I suddenly noted a profound shift in my psyche as I began to feel as she had felt so long ago. It was as if I had dropped into an ongoing story with no beginning and no visible end.

. . .

It was late in the day as I rode my good horse down by the shore of Collingham's lake to watch the setting sun. This lake had always been my passion and my friend. She was mine from earliest remembrance, and I shared her with no one. None of the people living round about had reason to go there, so I was startled to see a woman at the end of the jetty. Tall and slender and covered in a long cape, she stood looking toward the setting sun. I rode my horse down to the edge of the sand. The way she stood there, so still, gazing out across the water made her seem alone, proud and powerful in a mysterious way. Something kept me from running down the jetty to speak to her.

She did not turn to look at me; I do not know if she even saw me. I sat down quietly on a little grassy patch near the sand, my horse grazing beside, and watched her. She stood like a statue in the encroaching darkness. The only movement was from her cloak blowing gently in the evening breeze, its grayness blending with the fog and mist that began to rise from the water. I was fascinated by this woman. I knew that I had never seen her before; she did not look like a woman who lived nearby.

I stayed later than usual, until the sun was off the horizon. The red and orange sunset had faded from the sky, and darkness was near. I knew being out like this would cause me trouble at home, but I was eager to see what this woman would do, where she would go when she left the jetty.

I continued to stare out after her, into the moonlight, but I soon realized, with a start, that she was no longer there. She had not walked to the end of the jetty and gone down along the shore. I had been watching practically without blinking. She had not escaped my gaze, and I could not imagine where she had gone. An eerie feeling came over me. I stroked my horse's nose for comfort, mounted with a spring to my stirrup, and rode at a dead gallop back home.

My mother was summarily angry when I arrived, and she sent me to my bedchamber without a proper meal. I sat in the dark, looking out the window, watching the trees sway in the night breeze. I thought about the fog that had come in over the lake and about the strange lady who had seemed to fade away into the fog.

That night I dreamed that a woman was to become my teacher. I did not know what kind of a teacher she would be, but I did know that she was wise and kind and eager to help me. I sensed that my life was going to be difficult and that I would need her most dearly.

Why had I dreamed of such a woman? Who could she possibly be? Even stranger, why was she carrying a falcon on her arm, as my father did when he went out to hunt? I remembered the lady with the falcon I had seen on the hill. I could not imagine a woman handling falcons the way my father did. The thought of her was frightening, yet enthralling to me. I was entranced with the mystery surrounding this woman. Perhaps I was just making her up. Perhaps it was all just a dream. Maybe the woman I had seen standing on the jetty had never existed either.

I waited impatiently all day, thinking of nothing but riding my horse back to the lakeshore at sunset. I knew I could not stay as late as I had before, but I thought I might get a glimpse of her. This time I would go up to her and say a word or two.

Late that afternoon, after I had done all that was required of me, I went out to the stable and asked James the stableman to saddle my horse. He told me my horse was lame and said I had best not ride this day. For a moment I thought he was lying to me, that my mother had told him not to let me ride out alone. I ran into the stall and saw that indeed my horse was very sore. James said that it was a stone bruise. I was not to worry myself; he would be fine in a day or two, and I should leave him alone and let him heal.

I left the stable in a great flurry and hid against the walls of the house behind the bushes of heather so that no one would see me. I caught my breath and considered what to do. Maybe I could get to the lake without my horse. No one was near, so I ran down the road, out the gates, and out of sight. I knew I was going to have to run most of the way, lifting my skirts to my knee in a most unseemly manner, to get there in time, only to turn around and come back right away, but that was fine with me.

As I ran down the road, I suddenly remembered a path my father had shown me years past that led over Fletton's hill by the old Saxon tower. I would be able to arrive at Collingham's lake a little sooner, perhaps, and see from what direction the woman came.

A half hour later I got to the top of Fletton's hill. The rubble of the ancient Saxon tower lay jagged against the sky like broken teeth. I had a view of nearly the whole of the lake. I looked around carefully for movement, but the lakeshore was deserted. I thought I should go home at once, but there was an urge of some kind inside me, an overwhelming pressure to keep going.

From the corner of my eye, I sensed movement on a hillside opposite. Looking in that direction, I saw the shadowy form of a woman standing proudly with her arm held up toward the sky. I realized by her posture that this was the lady I had seen by the lake. I heard a piercing scream as I watched a peregrine falcon circle down from the darkening blue sky to the woman's outstretched arm. She turned and disappeared into a light mist floating over the hill.

As the woman disappeared, I began to run after her. In minutes I reached the top of the hill where I had last seen her. Eagerly, I looked down the other side. For a moment I saw only a lush, verdant pasture and fog rolling in from the west. Then a movement and a splash of red caught the corner of my eye. The woman, falcon still perched on her arm, was walking around a low, cobbled wall toward a small, stone cottage at the end of a path. High flowers surrounded her, and finally several elms and alders obscured her from view. I started running down the hill. As I reached the path she had been on, I saw her enter the cottage and close the sky blue door behind her.

I ran up the path through a garden to the cottage. The hedges and surrounds were of roses and holly. I knocked at the door. It opened, and an old woman stood at the threshold. She wore her gray hair pulled back off her face, which was wrinkled but oblong and fair. She looked like someone's grandmother. Her eyes twinkled blue from underneath heavy lids.

"Grandmother, where is the wondrous woman that I followed here?" I asked, suddenly realizing how rude I was being.

She smiled at me and said, amiably composed, "My child, I have just made honey cakes. Will you come in and have one?"

I looked through the door, past the old woman standing in her long dark blue dress and white lace apron, at the pleasant room, expecting to see a falcon on its perch. But there was no falcon. A last ray of sunlight flowed in through the leaded windows. There was the smell of warm cakes in the air; my stomach moved, and I immediately became hungry. But I was mystified and a little frightened. I had seen the woman with the falcon pass through this door moments before. It was very strange, and despite my fear I was enthralled by the mystery of it all. As I looked at the old woman standing there smiling at me, my wide eyes betrayed my concern.

"Come, child, you seem afraid. Perhaps I can serve you in your trouble?" she said.

Tentatively, I walked into the cottage. She took my cloak and hung it on a peg on the back of the door. I went over to a very simple wooden table. There were cakes in a basket, and honey, and a pool of sunlight reflected from a silver knife. I sat down in an old wooden chair and—unreasonably—wanted to cry. I could not understand why I was so upset.

The old woman sat down across the table from me, and we ate honey cakes in a companionable silence. After a time, as if reading my thoughts, she said, "My child, you are troubled. There is no need. You are a very special and beautiful young girl. The world can be any way you want it to be."

I looked at her in wonder. She seemed wise and strong, but there was something else unexplainable, a kind of light around her body. Maybe it was just the effect of the late sun flooding in through the windows behind her.

"May I ask your name? My name is Catherine," I said.

"You may call me Grandmother. It is a pleasure to meet you, Catherine," the old woman said, a smile wrinkling her cheeks.

"Grandmother, is the mysterious woman with the falcon your daughter?" I asked, watching her face.

"As you can most plainly see, there is no woman or falcon in my tiny cottage. She must have gone into the forest," the old woman said. She handed me a honey cake, which I took happily.

"What brings pleasure to your life out here so far from anyone?" I asked.

"I grow flowers, and I guess you could call me a teacher."

"What do you teach about?"

The old woman smiled and looked away. Her eyes caught the rosy glow of the failing sun, and for a moment she looked years younger. There was an irresistible kindliness in her expression. I knew that I had, at long last, found a friend.

"Not to presume what is clearly before your eyes, but I teach about life and truth," she finally said, looking directly into my eyes.

"Will you teach me?" I asked eagerly.

"Are you sure that truth is something you want to know about?"

"Yes, if it would make me grow up to be like you!"

The old woman laughed as she glanced out the window at the sunset. After a long pause, she spoke to me seriously. "Remember this, my child. Yes, I will teach you, but you must never tell anyone about our work together, for it is a sacred secret. For reasons yet unknown to you, I trust you, because I know of your spirit, even though we are strangers. Although you are still a maiden, you have the spirit of a woman, and you are a woman with great heart.

"I send you home now, my child. It is getting late. I wish you good dreams this night, and when you arrive home, everything will be to your liking. Do not be of fearful mind. Go on with your life as you always have, and when you need to see me, I will be here, always ready to serve you. Bless you, my child," she said and kissed me on top of my head.

I walked out the door, wrapped my cloak about me against the chill, and began to run home along the path. My mind was buzzing with this new encounter, and most of all I was excited because I had a friend. I felt as though my whole life had changed, as if I were suddenly waking up. I had a new reason for living, and although I did not know clearly what that reason was, I knew that this old woman had answers for me. And I had so many questions!

CHAPTER · 4

DESCENDING
THE
DREAM

A BLAST OF COLD AIR on my face awakened me from my dreaming. I opened my eyes, and Agnes was kneeling beside me. In her hand was her beautiful beaded fan. She was dusting my face with the long feathers. The current of cold air had come from the opening door. Ruby had just entered and was sitting at the other side of me, a quizzical look on her face.

"Well," she said.

I looked at Ruby and just shook my head. I looked at Agnes, and I could not find the words to describe what had happened to me. "Agnes, you are so much like the woman, the grandmother, in my dreaming," I said, as I took off the necklace with great care.

Agnes chuckled to herself and offered me a piece of jerky. "What woman are you speaking of, Little Black Wolf?" she asked.

"I'm sorry. I'm talking about the woman in my dreaming. I feel as if you have been with me, both you and Ruby."

"See? There you go running off and not telling us what you are doing," Ruby said in a huff. "Why don't you take us with you? That would certainly be the kind thing to do."

"But Ruby, I feel as if you are already with me in my heart when I come back here to this Dreamlodge. In a sense it's the same place, although it looks different."

"Oh, really," Ruby said, looking at me as though I had lost my mind. "Well, I guess you can fool some people with that kind of talk, but you certainly can't fool me."

"Why don't you let me get my feet on the ground and wake up a bit, Ruby, before you get all angry with me?"

"Well, how would you feel if you were always left behind?" Ruby said.

"I wouldn't feel good about it, Ruby, but you know I'm not leaving you behind. If I could take you with me in my dreams, I would."

"Well, you can," Ruby said with a sly look.

"But Ruby, I can hardly take myself. How can I take anyone else? I haven't learned how to do that," I said.

Agnes clucked her tongue at Ruby and shook her head. "Little Wolf has not learned how to dream with us yet, but she will soon, perhaps not in this journey, but maybe in the next one."

"Well, I sure wish she would learn a bit faster," Ruby said disgustedly. "Come, Lynn, it is time for breakfast. You must be very hungry. Go into the cabin. We will eat. Then, perhaps, you can tell us of this wonderful dream journey that you have been taking."

"You mean I missed dinner?" I asked.

"Yes, I'm afraid so," Ruby said. "I even had to do the dishes, and you know what that means."

Agnes laughed. "Yes, you missed dinner, but it is time to get up. You have been dreaming long enough. Come."

I got up very slowly from the sheepskins and placed the necklace carefully above the altar. I was stiff, and even though I was wrapped in robes, I felt very cold. Agnes and Ruby turned me around to the four directions and smudged me with sweet grass, sage, and cedar. We all three took offerings to the fire, thanking the Great Spirit and Mother Earth for my journey. We left the Dreamlodge, closed the flap behind us, and walked up the trail along the creek back to the cabin.

There was smoke coming out of the cabin's chimney. I took a deep breath and shook my head to clear it. Part of me was still in that green landscape with the oak trees. For a moment I looked for the lake and my horse. I was disoriented—and suddenly very sick to my stomach. I looked up at the sky dark with heavy rain clouds. I felt a few raindrops on my face, and we began to run toward the cabin. By the time we reached the porch, the rain was coming down in sheets and being blown across our path in a torrent.

Inside the cabin it was cozy and dry. We stripped off our parkas and sat down at the table that stood next to the old wood-burning stove.

"Did you go back to the Yucatán?" July asked as she served us muffins and honey and tea.

For a moment I didn't know what she was talking about. Then I realized that she was asking if I had gone down to visit Jaguar Woman. I had once long ago followed the butterfly migration in my dreaming.

"No, July, this dreaming was not to go down and visit Jaguar Woman, Zoila, and José. My dreaming this time is back into a long-ago age. I don't really know how long ago it was because I didn't ask anybody what the date was," I said.

"What do you mean, a long-ago age?" July asked me, surprised.

"That's why we built the Dreamlodge," Agnes said.

"Oh, now I understand," July said.

"Yes, July, a Dreamlodge is used for dreaming," Ruby said, smiling at her as she poked July's ribs.

"I guess that is pretty obvious," July said. "I didn't realize that you would use the lodge to dream separately from sleeping."

We all started to laugh at July's confusion, and July laughed with us, shaking her head.

"I must say, July, I am as confused as you are," I said. "I don't quite understand what is happening, and I'm hoping that when we have finished breakfast, we can all talk. I need to understand this better."

"That's what we are all here for," Ruby said.

"Yes, thank you, Ruby," I said, handing her a muffin and a spoonful of honey.

"Where is that currant jam I like?" Ruby asked impatiently.

"We don't have any more currant jam," Agnes said.

"I don't know why you would give an old blind lady honey. Don't you see it is getting all over me? My fingers are getting sticky, and I don't like it," Ruby said.

Ruby was rubbing furiously at her fingers, which she used to catch drips of honey that were dribbling down her chin. She bounced up and down like an impatient little girl. I couldn't help but laugh at her antics. I didn't know whether she was teasing or not.

"Well, thanks a lot, Lynn. I'm glad I'm an object of fun for you, but I don't enjoy this one bit! If you had any respect for your elders, you would find me some currant jam."

"But you heard Agnes. We're out of currant jam, and actually, it's not jam anyway. It's jelly."

"Whatever it is, it's better than this stuff. I don't think it's very nice of you, Lynn. Every time you come here we are always having trouble," Ruby said.

"Ruby, your having honey has nothing to do with me."

"Oh, yes it does."

"Well, how do you figure?"

"Agnes always saves the honey and brings it out when you're here because she knows you like it. Otherwise, we would never have to have any of this nasty, sticky stuff."

Agnes got up from the table, picked up the honey, put it away on the shelf, and came back and sat down. Ruby was looking around for something, slapping at the table with the palms of her hands.

"Ruby, what is it now?" Agnes said.

"Well, I can't eat this muffin without anything on it," Ruby said.

"But you have a little butter on it," July said.

"You impertinent young lady," Ruby said to July. "I am not going to eat this muffin without anything on it." Now Ruby was sitting in her chair with her shoulders hunched and her chin jutting out like an old crone.

Agnes looked at Ruby and said, shaking her head, "Ruby, what can we do to make you happier? Just tell us, and we will try to do it."

"Just never mind, Agnes. If I don't matter to you, if you don't care whether I get any currant jam, that's just fine with me. Just neglect me. I don't care. Lynn is the guest of honor."

"Ruby, you are being quite unfair," I told her.

"Great. Now you think I'm being unfair. Well, that's the thanks I get for all I've done for you. You can just forget the whole thing. I don't even care where you have been on your journey. I really don't care. In fact, I'm going to leave right now."

Ruby stood up angrily from the table. She walked quickly across the cabin floor and opened the door. A blast of cold air and rain drenched her before she could slam the door. She turned around and said, "I see. You want to send me out there so I can drown, thank you very much."

"Here, Ruby, I have the perfect answer. There is a little bit of raspberry jam left. Would that make you happy?" July asked after rummaging through the cupboard.

"Well, that certainly is better than honey. Yes, that would be fine. Thank you, and no thanks to you, Lynn." Ruby sat back down, soaking wet, and took a big bite from the muffin. A smile was restored to her face.

Ruby happy again, we discussed my physical reactions on coming out of the Dreamtime, my coldness and how that was a natural reaction for the body being separated from its spirit and astral energy or heat. But mostly we discussed how I, as Catherine, could understand words in an early form of English that I had never heard. It constantly amazed me, how I could understand events and things on a visceral level. Agnes explained that one's spirit shield is imprinted with information that relates to personal patterns of growth and spirit evolvement. This imprinting is recorded on the spirit shield and remembered from one lifetime to another, once you have been initiated. She explained that the actual name Sisterhood of the Shields was chosen because shield, in a metaphorical sense, is another description of spirit that lives on forever.

After talking for some time about my dream journey, we went to bed. I slept well that night and woke up early and wrote for several hours in my journal. Agnes and I went to the Dreamlodge in the early afternoon. We gathered wild blue and yellow flowers in the horse pasture and placed them on the "face of the earth," my altar in the lodge, before I put on the necklace and lay down to begin my dream work.

I was beginning to see that I would simply enter into my past life at random. I would not reenter exactly where I had left off. Agnes said that there was no explaining this phenomenon. There was not a long time lapse, but always some shift in circumstances.

CHAPTER 5

FEAR
OF THE
UNKNOWABLE

GRANDMOTHER AND I walked out behind her old stone cottage. We sat on two chairs bleached white with age in a brightly colored flower garden that had obviously been cared for very lovingly for many years. It was early afternoon, and I had come straight to the old woman's house as soon as I could get away.

"What are you so nervous about, my child?" Grandmother asked.

"Grandmother, there is something about secrets, about not being able to tell anyone about you. You are so important to me, and I want to share our friendship with everyone," I said.

The old woman looked at me with a twinkle in her eye.

"What is your fear, my daughter?"

I thought for several minutes, trying to figure out a way to describe the feeling of tension I had in my stomach.

"Well, Grandmother, I guess fear is a knot in your stomach. I feel apprehensive, full of anxiety for I don't know what."

"Are you afraid of something that will happen in the future, Catherine?"

"Yes, I guess you are right. I am afraid that I am going to get into trouble somehow for learning secret teachings."

"Look around you. Look at the flowers. See how beautiful they are. Look at the butterflies as they dance from one flower to another. Feel the soft wind on your skin. Feel its warmth. Feel the rays of the sun bathing your body with light. That is all there is, my child. That is the present. Whether you understand that fully now or not, that is really all there is. There is no past, and there is no future. There is only this moment that we share together."

I looked around at the flowers and felt the balmy air on my skin. I looked up at the sun shining down through the trees, and my body relaxed a little. I looked at Grandmother, whose eyes held such kindness.

"You know, Grandmother, it is foolish for me to be full of anxiety, because I have never been so happy."

"Perhaps you are afraid to be happy."

"It is just that I have been lonely for so long; I never really had anyone to talk to. I guess because I am so happy now, I realize that I have never been happy before."

"So tell me, Catherine, where do you feel this fear?"

"I feel fear like a sheet of tension down my back and like a fist in my stomach."

"Can you name that fear? Can you say what fear actually is, not just what it feels like, but what fear is?"

I sat for several minutes and realized that I did not have an answer for her.

"Fear is a part of the unknowable," Grandmother said, "part of the vast experience we cannot name, for much of our experience as human beings is unnameable. We talk around the feelings. We explain where and how we felt the feelings, but the feeling itself is part of the unknowable. It is something we cannot really touch.

"Close your eyes for a moment, and take a deep breath, Catherine. Try to find fear inside you. It will elude you. Close your eyes, and let us see if we can find this little rascal that is causing you so much difficulty."

I spent a long time in meditation with Grandmother. Fear was like a mad dog running around inside me. When I went to search for that fear inside my stomach, it ran up the back of my neck. When I moved my consciousness into the back of my neck, it ran down my back, and I could not find it. Finally, when I cornered that mad dog back in my stomach again, I looked hard and could see nothing. At that point I opened my eyes. I told Grandmother what had happened.

She smiled. "Catherine, the nature of fear is unexplainable, because it is not really there."

"How can that be, Grandmother, when I can feel it?"

"No, my daughter, fear is elusive and hides from you, but it is not part of the present. When you say that you are afraid of what will happen to you as a result of knowing me and having this secret friendship, what are you really afraid of?"

"I am afraid that someone will find out."

"Who?" Grandmother asked.

"I am afraid that my parents will find out, and I will get into trouble."

"See," Grandmother said, "that is part of the future, is it not?"

"Yes," I said.

"When you think about the past and how much trouble you have been in before, that is something that is not in the present either. So you see, when you make yourself present, and you sit with yourself in meditation and go within yourself, fear disappears. It cannot exist under scrutiny at all."

Grandmother left her chair and went inside the little stone house and came back with a tray of oat bread for us. She said nothing, but I watched her careful movements. Everything she did was done with grace and perfection. I have noticed that when people do something that is a chore, they become very impatient. When Grandmother did things, she did them with great care, wasting no movements. Even to watch her do something as simple as serving the bread was satisfying.

"Grandmother, I love watching you prepare the bread for us."

"Thank you, Catherine. Why is it that you enjoy this so much?"

"Because your movements are so beautiful. Because you are so careful with things. Because you do not waste any time. Oh, Grandmother, I appreciate you very much. Thank you for being my friend."

Grandmother smiled and said nothing. As I watched the sunlight play on her face, I could have sworn that she grew much younger right before my eyes. She looked for a moment like a very young girl. The way she threw her head when a butterfly landed on her hair was not the movement of an old woman. But I said nothing and just watched, enjoying the companionship of my new friend.

The rest of the afternoon we said very little. I sat with Grandmother in the dirt, while she furrowed the ground and planted new seeds for her summer flowers. The current between us was wordless. Every once in a while a butterfly would come down and fly first around her head and then around mine and then fly away.

I learned much from watching Grandmother. She had a way of using her fingers. Now and again she would hand me a stone and have me hold it first in my left hand and then in my right. Then she would ask me to close my eyes and listen to the stone and see if the stone had anything to tell me. It might say it was male or female. More often than not, the stone would tell me something about my life. One time a brown jagged stone reminded me exactly of my father and his sharp temper. I would give the stone back to the old woman, and she would place it where she found it.

Later that afternoon, just as I was about to leave, Grandmother reached into her pocket and took out a clear quartz crystal. It was very small, faceted on one end, and very smooth, as if it had been polished. She handed it to me.

"I want you to take this home with you and place it under your pillow."

"I would love to do that, Grandmother, but tell me why."

"I want you to learn to dream."

"But I dream a good deal already."

"No, there is dreaming, and then there is dreaming."

"But I do not understand."

"Place the crystal under your pillow tonight, and remember your dream. Perhaps when you awaken in the morning you will have had a very special experience. I want you to write down enough of it so that you can remember what to tell me when next you see me. This crystal is from Danu, the Divine Mother, the Old One. In this aspect, and she has many, she is benign. You have also experienced her more mysterious side as the lakeside enchantress, the insatiable one."

"You mean the woman I was intrigued by down by Collingham's lake?"

"Yes, Catherine. But Danu's crystal will bring you contentment and new learning."

"What will I do if someone finds the crystal, Grandmother?"

"Is it not possible that you could have found the crystal on your own, Catherine?"

"Oh, I imagine so."

"Well, tell them it was a gift from the earth. That is true."

I gave Grandmother a big hug, and she kissed me on the forehead. I pulled my cape around me, because the sun was now covered by clouds and it was much cooler outside. I left the garden of the little stone house and walked quickly down the road toward home.

When I arrived home, I went to my bedchamber and placed my crystal under my pillow. That night I fell asleep almost immediately, for I was very tired. I dreamed of the woman I had seen on the jetty. I had not been to the lake for some time now, but I immediately recognized her in my dreams. She was standing in a clearing high on a hill working with her falcon. I watched from below. She was holding her arm, wrapped with leather, up to the sky. With a shriek, the falcon swooped down and landed on her arm. Then the woman turned in my direction, and lifting the great bird high, she sent him toward me. He circled me several times, flying sunwise. The whole dream did not take very long, but it made a great impression on me because of its stark reality. When I awoke in the morning, I did not need to write it down. I knew I would never forget it.

THE
AWAKENING
OF A
FRIEND

The lady of whispers
seeks an opening which only I can give her
only having forgotten a key.
The night disguises itself in a wind of reason.

I HAD ARRIVED AT Grandmother's house one afternoon to find a young girl near my own age. Her name was Anne Hornby, and she was the old woman's granddaughter. She had come from down Durham's road to visit for a few days. She was a nice girl, and we became instant friends. Because the Hornbys were distant cousins of my father, I could tell my family that I was going to visit Anne, and they would not be concerned about why I kept going to the old woman's house.

One day I arrived in the early afternoon to find Anne doing some work in the garden for Grandmother. I had told my parents that Anne had asked me to spend the evening. They were not sorry to be rid of me, as they had important guests.

After Anne and I talked for a while, I walked into the stone cottage from the garden and saw Grandmother sitting at her table doing some embroidery. I gasped in amazement. She was surrounded by an intense light that looked like flames undulating in and out of the shadows. I could not speak. Grandmother raised her eyes to meet my stare. The look on her face was deeply intense, and she was not smiling. Slowly, as she looked at me, the flaming light around her subsided. She sat there, still holding her embroidery. The light from the window at her side now filled the room with only a gentle glow.

"Sit, my daughter, and close your mouth." I did, a little nervous, and sat down at the table across from her.

"Grandmother, I saw a flame of light all around you and within you. What was that?"

Grandmother laid her needlework on the table. "There is something called a spirit shield. I told you once, Catherine, that there were great healers from the ancient teachings of Wyrrd. Did it ever occur to you that perhaps I am a healer?"

"Well, I had not put it in those words, but yes, Grandmother, it had occurred to me that you seem to have unusual abilities—now I *know* you do. Is what I saw part of being a healer?"

"What you just saw was a spirit shield. There is spirit in all things. There is spirit in the rocks, in the trees, in the earth, in people and animals, and in our wondrous flying friends."

"But Grandmother, the Church teaches that only people have a spirit, and those people must be God's people in the Church," I said.

After several moments of silence, Grandmother looked up at me from under her eyelids. "And what did you feel about that?"

"I never understood it, because how can the trees and animals be less alive than we are?"

"I have been taught that all of life is part of God, or Danu. Danu is love and light, and we are reflections of that great light. Danu is sometimes darkness, and sometimes we also reflect that aspect of her."

"But I have never seen light around a person the way I just saw it around you, except as I told you, once when I was a child," I said, twisting in my chair.

"You saw more light around me, my daughter, because you are beginning to see better. You are beginning to learn. I wanted you to see the light around me, because I want to teach you something today."

"About light? About those flames I saw around you?"

"Yes, Catherine, I want to teach you about what that is, and one day you will be able to create light around yourself. You have light around you now, but you have no control over it."

"What is the light made of?" I asked.

"The light source is spirit, and the intensity of it has to do with the strength of your own power."

"What do you mean by power, Grandmother?"

"When I talk about power with you, I am not talking about your having the sort of power over anyone that the king or the Church has. I am talking about personal power, your ability to make alive in the world your own dream."

"My father has power like that."

"Yes, I am sure that he does, but probably your father does not know how to use that ability to heal others."

"Do you mean healing the body of diseases?"

"Yes, I am speaking of that, but that is not exactly the way that I work, so I am not going to teach you in exactly that way. I am going to teach you about making yourself strong, so the possibility of diseases, the possibility of unrest and unhappiness, does not arise in your life."

"I could certainly use training like that; I need it most clearly. But what is the spirit shield? Is it part of the soul?"

"The spirit shield exists between the soul and the physical body. The spirit shield is a tool in the way of Wyrrd."

"What is the way of Wyrrd?"

"There is a power in the universe that can be used and learned about. There is a whole world, Catherine, that you have seen only a glimpse of. When you see light around living things, when you know what events are about to happen, when you talk to the birds—that is part of the world of Wyrrd. It is the world of Danu that you do not see. It is the unknowable world."

"But, Grandmother, how can I know an unknowable world?"

"You can understand the effects of the unknowable—you can see

Danu rising out of the lake mists at dawn—but you cannot understand how that happens. I can only show you the flames of light around my being, and you can sense the power of that, but I cannot explain it. We call it the arousal of the inner fire. I can lead you there. You can sense the warmth of Danu's smile or feel her wrath as the menacing sea witch. I can help make you strong."

"But how can you do that, Grandmother? How can you make me strong? I want to be stronger."

"I teach you to be strong by helping you to unlearn many things you think are true."

"Oh," I said, still confused and a little disappointed at her words, but I remained silent.

"The way of Wyrrd is about power. It is about understanding energy and the flow of energy, seeing the many faces of the Mother Goddess. Energy has been understood for thousands of years, but very few people possess this knowledge, because they are frightened of it."

"Why are they frightened, Grandmother? Does it hurt them?"

"No, it does not hurt them. Only their fear hurts them. What they are afraid of is the ignorance of the people around them. People do not understand what they are saying. People do not know the importance of understanding energy. Energy flows like Brixworth's river. You can float on the currents like an alder leaf. From the beginning of time there have been certain gifted people who have understood life and its flows, and they gave it a name. They called it energy, but they could not explain what it was. They just knew that they felt it, and they knew that they could use it to heal. When Jesus healed all those people in the Scriptures, he was using energy. He was a great magician of Wyrrd. He was someone who cared about the balance of the earth. He cared about what was true. He cared about healing people, and he did it with his personal power. And so they called him the son of God. He was so far beyond the understanding of most people that even though they called him God and saw him do miraculous things, the people murdered him."

"I have never understood that, Grandmother. If he was such a healer and he did so many good things, why would they crucify him?"

"Well, I think they crucified him because they did not understand him, and what we do not understand we want to destroy. That is the human tragedy, and that is what I want to train you to understand. I want you to be able to become the most magnificent woman that you know how to be. I want to help you to be that. But you must never speak of this teaching. People will know that you are a wonderful woman, and maybe one day you will be able to quietly pass this teaching on to an apprentice as I am going to do with you."

"Grandmother, that's so exciting! I am so honored that you trust me. Thank you."

"Well, let us go on and talk about the spirit shield, Catherine."

Grandmother got up and got bread for us and handed me a small piece. She put her embroidery away, and we sat down. She picked up her piece of bread and took a delicate bite. I did the same. She watched me in silence for several minutes while we ate and smiled as I began to relax and enjoy myself.

"The spirit shield that you saw around me comes from the Creator. It comes from the Old One or God or the Mother Goddess—she has many names. Sometimes she is Danu the Goddess female, or sometimes the male Don, or neither male nor female. However you think of God is fine, but we, just between us, will call her the Old One for now. The spirit shield is a reflection of the Old One. It is the part of you that is always part of God. It is evidence of your power. It is your protection, and it actually is your power of Wyrrd.

"There are great sages, great men and women of wisdom who have lived in the mountains of Europe, high among the snowcapped peaks. They can sit in the snow, and they can melt the snow for many, many feet all around them. They can sit naked and never be cold because they have created an extraordinary heat within them. I will show you how to do that when the snows fall this winter. But now I will give you an exercise to center yourself and begin your work of building your power. Come with me into the garden."

We walked out into the beautiful garden. Anne had gone down to Brixworth's river to sit by the Eywas Cross; she was nowhere to be seen. Grandmother took me up to a beautiful elm tree and had me sit on the ground with my back to it. Then she placed four stones around me.

She said, "These are Danu's praying stones for the four directions. They are powerful mother stones, and they will help you. I want you to sit with your back to the tree breathing deeply from here." She poked her belly just below the navel. "That is the seat of your power. Breathe deeply and let yourself relax. Close your eyes. Feel your back up against the tree; feel the power of the tree. Feel the sap moving up and down the trunk. Actually feel the movement of the tree's sap, its life force. In the sap lives the spirit shield of the tree. I will leave you here now until you sense that. When you do, your exercise is over. Come back then and join me inside the house."

It took me many minutes to relax and get comfortable. Finally, I sat with my back to the bark of the tree, and I felt a coolness up and down my spine that slowly began to turn to heat. I did not know if my body was warming the tree or the tree was warming my body, but it did not matter.

I knew that the tree was welcoming me, and I felt that the tree appreciated the light I was giving to it, because as I sat with my eyes closed, I began to envision the tree enveloped in a whole cocoon of light that enveloped me also. And as I breathed slowly, the tree began to breathe with me.

I must have sat there for a very long time. I never opened my eyes. My concentration came very easily, and it was not long before I found a very peaceful and powerful center within my own being, a center I felt I would hold with me for the rest of my life. I realized that this tree was a great teacher. It was as if I heard nothing and began to lose the sense of my own body. I felt a oneness with the trunk of that tree until I could envision roots coming down through my legs into the earth. They went down very deep, all the way into middle earth. And as the tree gently swayed with the breeze, I would sway with her. I knew she was female and she was very old. And I knew also that I was not the first apprentice to work with this tree. I knew that this tree could teach me much, that she would give me messages, that she enjoyed me. I felt a great kinship with her.

But it was a long time before I could get a sense of the sap. Finally I felt a tingling coming up my right leg. At first I thought it was my leg going to sleep; then I realized that this tingling was moving up my leg and into my hip and along the right side of my spine. It moved up and up, very slowly. It must have taken an hour to go up my side. Then I felt the tingling across the top of my head and back down my left side. I knew that the sap that had gone up the tree was moving slowly. The energy was moving along the sap and coming back down my left side. It took at least another hour for me to complete the circle. I knew it was important. Something inside me knew that I was to wait until the circle was completed.

I finally opened my eyes, full of a new sense of myself. I felt as if I had broadened my understanding of the world in some inexplicable way. I had learned something from the tree. She spoke to me through the movement of her sap. I knew there was a language of the trees that I needed to learn.

It was almost dark outside, and I saw that someone had placed a blanket around me without my being aware of it. I had not had any idea that someone had approached me during my meditation. But as I woke up, I pulled the blanket around my shoulders and ran into the house. The lanterns were lit; Anne and Grandmother were sitting at the table doing embroidery work; and there was the smell of stew on the stove. I threw my arms around Grandmother, I was so excited.

"Grandmother, I felt the sap moving. And Grandmother, there is more," I said as I sat down. My face must have been full of excitement, because Grandmother and Anne laughed a little and poked each other as they watched me. "Grandmother, I know that there is a language in the trees. Am I right? They talk to one another, do they not?"

"Yes, Catherine, there is a language of the trees, and it is very ancient. I am glad you heard that. It is important that you learn that language."

"Yes, Grandmother, I know that, and I know that there is much wisdom in that tree. I thought it was an elm tree, but it is not, is it?"

"No, Catherine, it is an alder, and alders are very sacred trees."

"Yes, Grandmother, I know that. I do not know *why* I know that, but I feel it. I sense it. And I know that tree has taught many people before me. Is that so?"

"Oh, yes, she is a grandmother; she has been around a long time, almost as long as I have." Grandmother chuckled and patted me on the top of the head. "You are a good girl, Catherine. You did well today, and I am proud of you. Are you hungry now?"

"Oh, yes, Grandmother, I am starving." Anne got up and got plates for everyone. "I can help you, Anne."

"No, that is all right. I think it is important that you talk to Grandmother right now." She went to get us our dinner.

Grandmother looked at me for a long time, neglecting the embroidery in her lap. She said nothing. Finally she said, "Are there any questions you need to ask?"

"Grandmother, how is it that I know some of these things? I do not understand that."

"Well, my child, perhaps it is because you have lived before."

"But Grandmother, what do you mean?"

"I mean that there is a chance—this is something for you to think about and perhaps ask the tree—there is a chance that you have been on this earth before but in a different time. Maybe you have learned these things before, and maybe our work together is only a process of remembering what you have already known. That is possible, Catherine."

"You mean that I might have been a stone before or maybe a tree or a horse?"

"Well, some say that is possible, Catherine. It is also possible that you have been a human being before."

"Oh, I see. You mean I could have been a boy in another life," I said with surprise.

"Yes, it is possible," Grandmother said, laughing. "It is important to learn what it is like to be a man, and it is important to learn what it is like to be a woman to be balanced in our spirit, that spirit shield we were talking about. Sometimes it takes more than one lifetime to build that spirit shield and make it powerful."

"I see, Grandmother." Now I felt confused.

Grandmother, reading my thoughts, said, "My child, do not be confused. You have much to learn, and this is only the beginning. Relax, here is some embroidery work for you to do. Anne tells me that you are very good at that." I blushed.

"Yes, I have been told that I do embroidery very well, but I must tell you, Grandmother, that I do not like to do embroidery. And if there is anything else you would like me to do, I would rather do that. I will do anything other than embroider. But if you want me to do it, I will."

"I understand. It does not matter what you do, but I want you to do something with your hands. It is important right now."

Grandmother handed me some knitting, which I really did not want to do. I picked it up and looked at the stitches and began.

"Wizards and the power people of Wyrrd always knew each other by the spirit shield. They could see the flames around another wizard's body, and they would know of that wizard's power," Grandmother said as we sat there working.

We had a wonderful dinner together, and I began getting sleepy. But Grandmother just talked casually to Anne and me as if she were talking about making preserves. She talked in simple words about the wonders of the universe and the mysteries of things untold.

"Anne, I want you to put down your embroidery. I want you to collect yourself, and I want you to put heat into your hands as best you can."

For many minutes Anne sat quietly with her eyes closed, breathing in and out in short breaths. Finally she reached out her palms toward me.

"Catherine, I ask you to place your hands about an inch above Anne's hands, and I want you to tell me what you feel."

I put down my knitting and placed my palms an inch above Anne's palms. They were hot, as if they had been in hot, boiling water. I caught my breath. I looked at Grandmother in astonishment.

"Grandmother, her hands are hot like a fire."

"Now take your hands away, and look at Anne."

As I looked at Anne, I began to see a vague light or glow around her, particularly around her hands. They were glowing in the dark, bluish yellow light.

"Oh, Grandmother, how can she do that? Anne, can you teach me how to do that?"

"I do not know how to teach you how to do this, Catherine, but I am glad that you can see it, because it is also a gift to be able to see it. Not many people can."

"Is that true, Grandmother?"

"Yes, it is true, and I too am happy that you can see how much work

Anne has done. She is very smart and a very good girl, and she does this very well. She will be a great healer one day, and I do think that you will be friends for much longer than you know."

Anne got up and relit the lanterns. I sat at the table, stunned at what I had just seen.

"You know, Grandmother, it is wonderful to experience these things, because I know that they are true. Yet if I have not really seen something, there is still a part of me that doubts. But now that I have seen this for myself, more than just hearing the words, I know that it is true, and I know that one day I will be able to do this as well."

"And how do you know that, Catherine?"

"Because if she can do it, I can do it. I know I can."

"Yes, Catherine, but you may do it in a different way. There is one thing that you must remember. You have made a bid for power, even though you do not know that. Your whole life has been a journey toward discovery, a journey toward wisdom. That is what sets you apart from other girls, from other people. But power must come to you. It is a gift. And for power to come to you, you must make a place within yourself for that power to live. It must have a home within you. Your fear will keep power away, your fear of what people might say, your fear of being revealed as a witch. You must be very careful, and I cannot stress this enough. You are not doing any of this to show off or make power over people to hurt them or to control anyone at all, ever. This teaching is for your own evolvement as a soul. We are talking about enlightenment, Catherine. We are talking about becoming, one day, one of the wise ones."

"Do you mean like the old ones who sit in the snow in the mountains?"

"Well, I mean *like* them, but I do not think that is what you are going to do. There is a circle, a council you might call it, that you cannot see, that is not part of this world. But it is part of this world in that it is connected to you through your spirit shield. It is a circle that you belong to, and in this lifetime or maybe in other lifetimes, you will find your way back to that circle. And when you do, you will know that you have come home. There is a yearning inside you, a need deep in your heart. You want to go back to the people who understand you. Those people are the wise ones, the extraordinary beings that exist on other levels of consciousness."

"Oh, Grandmother, I do not know what you mean, other levels of consciousness."

"It is part of the unknowable, Catherine. It is part of Danu's world — the land of the Old One. The other levels of consciousness have to do with the higher part of yourself, that part of yourself that knows all, the part of yourself that already has all wisdom, because it is part of Danu or of God, and God is all wisdom and all knowing."

"Do you mean, Grandmother, that I am part of God?"

"Well, in a sense you are. When we teachers try to explain these things to an apprentice we are slowed down by language. There is no language to describe the transformation of a person into the world of Wyrrd. We have to use words that so often have different meanings than what we intend, so if you are confused, I understand that. But just know that there is a circle of old ones that watches over you, that is calling you back, and you will find your way there some day. I am here to help you to do that."

Not long after, I gathered my things and left for home.

CHAPTER · 7

A
MIRROR
OF
POWER

Even the ones who will not read
listen for the sound echoing
out of the forest.
We are too far away
for the night to do us harm.
The night used to soothe us.
With lights we have removed
the outer world and we must
face our shadowy minds
instead.

I RETURNED THE NEXT day and sat outside in the garden with my teacher. She was resting. Yellow daisies grew in tangled clumps in a circle around our chairs, and pink roses lent their perfume to the warm air. After a time, Grandmother opened her eyes and looked at me with a little twinkle and a smile. "Have you ever had dreams, Catherine, about the stars?"

"Well, I guess I have. I have had one dream many different times; it is about a beautiful being, a woman, who comes down from the stars and sits on my bed at night and talks to me. She says that she is from the Star Nation, that she is my protector. She used to come when I was very young, when my father was away and my mother was ill and I was often alone. She used to come and keep me company through the long nights. She taught me many things. She taught me about the elves. She called them star children. She taught me about the animals. She said the birds were from the Bird Nations and that they were tribes, and the birds loved me and would protect me. When I asked her where she was from, she would take me over to the window and point to the stars."

There was a look in Grandmother's eyes that I had never seen before. It was very intense; her eyes looked like deep, black pools. She stared at me until I became uncomfortable.

"Grandmother, why are you looking at me that way?"

"I am sorry, Catherine. I was trying to see deeply into the light around you. You have a different light around you when you talk about this woman from the stars. You have not mentioned her before, and I am glad that you have met her. It will make our work together much easier."

"Why is that, Grandmother?"

She shook her head, not wanting to answer me. Instead she got up and motioned for me to get up and we moved indoors. She brought us some cheese and bread and sat down across from me at the table.

"Have you ever traveled to the stars?" she asked.

"Why no, Grandmother, I did not know anyone could travel to the stars. But I did have a dream once that the stars were very close to me and that they had fallen down from the sky and landed on my cloak and in my hair. They sparkled like diamonds all around me. What do the birds have to do with the stars, anyway?"

"A long time ago," Grandmother said, "I was sitting down by Collingham's lake. It was early morning, and I saw a faerie spirit come across the water. I had been sitting with a rattle I had been using to talk to the faeries of the lake. The rattle that I used was ancient; it had been used by my grandmother and her grandmother before her to call the energies of

Danu together. Those energies I call the faeries of the water. Then the faeries came and took my rattle. I looked down in my lap where it had been resting, and it was no longer there. I looked everywhere for that rattle, because it was very sacred and precious to me. I was angry at these faeries, because I thought it was very unkind of them to take something so sacred to me and hide it.

"I went back to the lake after several days, and I sat in the same place, and I asked for the faeries to come and talk to me and tell me why they had done such a thing. I saw the faeries come across the waters again, and this time they surrounded me, and I felt a coolness and a dampness on my cheeks. Suddenly a bolt of lightning came down out of the sky and thundered into the ground in front of me. Within that thunderbolt, that golden blast of light, I saw a vision. I saw the faeries of the lake that had come to me, but this time in the form of a deer. That deer walked around me four times, honoring the four directions of Danu, and then asked me to follow it.

"I followed it into the water, and it took me down to the bottom of the lake. It showed me the sacred herbs and plants that grow there. And we ate together, the deer and I, the deer grazing on the plants, giving me a leaf here and there to chew on. And these leaves healed my heart, and I was no longer filled with sadness about my rattle.

"Then the deer curled up next to me, and the spirit of the deer spoke to me and said that the spirit of the rattle was asleep, that I must not grieve over the loss of the rattle because it would be a long slumber; there was nothing I could do at this time. It was not appropriate for me to have the rattle because the spirit of the rattle was in a deep, dark sleep. That spirit would dream me, and from time to time lessons would come. The spirit of the deer said that people would come for me to share my knowledge with and that they would be from the stars.

"Then the spirit of the deer told me that the sapphires inside the rattle were from the star people who had been here three hundred thousand years ago. Because of the pain on Mother Earth, because of the deception and the disorder and the disharmony, the spirit of the rattle had to go to sleep, and when harmony was restored on the planet, the rattle would then be restored to me, because I am the Keeper of the Star Rattle.

"Then I followed the deer out of the lake and back to the place where I had been sitting. The deer circled me four times and then disappeared. I felt a warm wind circle me, then leave me, and I watched the faeries cross the surface of the water and disappear into Geddington's forest."

Grandmother looked across at me. I was wide-eyed with fascination. She said, "Catherine, you have been brought to me by the spirit of the Star Rattle. You are here because you were meant to be here. All of your lives have led to your being here. There are no mistakes in life, and we can learn much from each other. We have much to give each other, and we should rejoice that the spirits have made it possible. You must not doubt. Do not doubt that you are the magnificent human being that you are. You are special. Do not let the world take away your power. You cannot fight the ignorance in people. They have more strength than you in the physical world, but they do not know your spirit, nor do they even understand the meaning of spirit. As you grow you will become an example of light and others will become more aware because of it. You are in a war against ignorance. You are a warrioress, and you hold up your shield and your sword as surely as the sun comes up every day."

"Grandmother, your stories inspire me so! What you say I know in my heart is true, but I am reluctant to be different from everybody else. I do not want to be singled out. I do not want to be hurt. I am afraid. I cannot help but be afraid."

"Never mind, Catherine, you will learn not to be afraid. Fear is your only problem. We will learn to deal with fear, you and I. You are not alone. In fact there is a pantheon of light beings around you, elves, faeries, and old ones, and they are there to help you whether you ask them to or not. They will help to light your way."

"Grandmother, when are we going to begin these lessons you talk about?"

Grandmother chuckled to herself and ran her fingers over a dent in the table. Then she looked up at me. "Soon," she promised, "soon we will begin. A long time ago, Catherine, we were called the Power Holders of Wyrrd, and we believed and experienced the power of all life. We worshiped the firstness of woman. We believed that you can talk to the Bird Nations, to the four-leggeds. We believed that there is spirit in all things; if you listened carefully, you could talk to the stones, and they had many wise things to say.

"Then one day, one very dark day, there came a horde of men riding over the hill. They came and put us in chains, and then they questioned us. They wanted to know if we believed in their god. We said that we had never heard of their god. They beat us, then they questioned us again. They asked us if we believed in animals, the animal spirits. When we said yes, they beat us again, and they said that we were of the devil and we should all be killed. And almost all of us were."

I looked at Grandmother in awe, and whispered, "You were there? How did you escape?"

Grandmother had tears in her eyes. "They beat me until I was unconscious, and I lay on the floor for a very long time. They did not notice that I was still alive. I said nothing. I did not move until they were gone.

And when I did move, I got up, and I washed the blood off me, and I stood in my home — a home that was in shambles, that was completely destroyed — and I stood amid my family, all of them killed in the name of this new god. And I did not understand. I cried; I did not want to live. I was very young then, and I was filled with hatred and a need for revenge. These people had destroyed not only my family, but our entire world. Only a few of us survived, and we fled.

"We fled this time of great religious turmoil, and we hid in the mountains and by the lakes where no one could find us. We lived in caves, and no one knew we were alive. In fact, you are the first person I have ever told this story to, and I trust that you will never speak of this to anyone. But it is important for you to know that I can understand your pain, that it is real to me, that when I smile and I laugh at you, it is not because I am making light of your feelings. I want to help you feel better and stronger. I want to bring laughter and light into your life. You must understand that there is much destructive ignorance in the world.

"It took me many years to learn that their god was a being of light, that these people who destroyed everyone and everything I knew truly did not understand what they were doing. I believe that this holy man would never have wanted anyone to die for him. He is a messenger of God, just as all the beings on this earth are messengers of God. It is important that you understand this. I do not believe that this god taught right and wrong as the Church teaches. What is sacred is sacred, and what is is, and all things that are on this planet are sacred. There is no wrong or right in that sense. There is only God. And that is your first lesson, my daughter."

CHAPTER · 8

THE
SHADOW
WORLD

I SWEPT BACK THE FLAP of the doorway to my Dream-
lodge and looked outside at the clouds above. It had been raining, and the
clouds were gray-blue. Behind them, pieces of sky peeked through in
pink and orange and turquoise blue. The layers of clouds, one upon another, were like the layers of consciousness that I had been traveling. I
turned to Agnes, who was still sitting by the fire. I had come out of the
dream thirty minutes before, but I was unable to speak. After doing several breathing exercises with Agnes, I had finally been able to move and
stand up.

"Agnes," I said slowly, my voice a little husky, "I am still having trouble understanding what this process is that I am doing. I am dreaming, yet
I'm not asleep. Can you explain that?"

I looked back at the clouds as they began to shred like thin cotton
being pulled apart.

"We have spoken together of doubling," Agnes replied. "Doubling
occurs in the physical."

"You mean when you are in one place and you can appear physically in
another place at the same time."

"That is approximately what it means," Agnes said. "There is no way
to explain these things in a rational language, because they are, again, part
of the shadow world, part of the unknowable. But as closely as I can explain it to you in words, you could be here — and if your intent and your
spirit intention were strong enough — you would be able to be here physically with me and still manifest the form of your body somewhere else. It
would not be your physical body, but someone could see you and think it
was your physical body. Now what you're doing in the Dreamlodge here
is different," she said.

I closed the flap to the Dreamlodge and went back to sit near Agnes,
next to the fire. "What do you call what I'm doing?" I asked.

"It is called doubling in the Dreamtime or dreamwalking. You are not
exactly just dreaming. You are actually sending your consciousness into a
separate time, so that you are not moving in the astral but beyond it. You
must remember that when you move out of this physical, dualistic existence, you are moving away from the reference of the time-space relativ-
ity that we experience here." Agnes patted the floor of the Dreamlodge
with the palms of her hands. "We are moving out of time. That is why,
when you are working in the astral, it is impossible to tell what time it is.
What you are doing when you dreamwalk, Lynn, is moving into history,
into the past. You are exploring your lifeline. When you leave your body,
you are going down your cord, which has existed through your many life-

times and has been created by your spirit connection with the Great Spirit."

"You mean to tell me that there is an actual cord that leads from each of my lives to the next?"

"Yes, my daughter, it leads from one lifetime to another until it goes full circle. It isn't going from beginning to end but full circle."

"Then do we just go on forever in that circle, reliving our lives?"

"You don't exactly relive your lives. You become a dreamwalker. Physical existence is structured to teach you things through the possibility of mirrors. You create your mirrors during a physical existence in this body that you are: you gather a family; you gather a husband, friends, a teacher like myself. And you learn from us. You learn from the reflection that you see. We are mirrors for you. You chose us. You learn as much as you're capable of learning. You have all that you need in this lifetime to become enlightened; whether that happens or not is really up to you."

"Everyone has the chance to become enlightened in one lifetime?" I asked.

"Yes, everyone has that opportunity. Everyone has what he or she needs, the mirrors. Each of us has asked, before being born, for everything needed. The problem is, when we are born, we become caught in the dream. We are born into a kind of sleep. To become enlightened is to wake up from that dream. It's not unlike waking up in the Dreamlodge and finding Catherine gone and me here."

I nodded in agreement. "I hear your words, Agnes, and I know what you say is true. Somewhere inside me it resonates truth to me. I know it's true, although I have no other memory of actually experiencing different lives. I don't remember my deaths, but I must say that I have a strong sense that my work with you has been a process of remembering. When you talk about doubling, dreamwalking, power, many times I intuitively know what you are going to say before you say it."

"When I first met you, Little Wolf, I told you this. I said that if you became my apprentice your learning with me would be a process of remembering, and that is true, is it not?"

"Yes," I said. "And you know, Agnes, when I am working in this dream, doubling in the dream as Catherine, I remember what has happened to her. I think that if I were put to the task of writing the rest of her story, I would have a pretty good idea of what happens."

"Yes, Lynn, I imagine that is true. Nevertheless, it is important for you to go through that experience slowly as it is revealed to you, because some of what is going to happen will be painful. Some will be ecstatic. You don't want to rush yourself. The cord is very sensitive. It is not that it is weak or that it is possible to break it, because it cannot be broken, but that hoop of your lives is indeed sensitive. Retracing those hoops is not an ordinary movement for any of us. We don't usually do that until we reach the end of our circling. And when I say the end, that is not really the way it is, but it is the only way I can describe it to you. You at some point finish the dance. Then you stand in the center of your circle with your lives around you, and you are no longer dreamwalking. Having encountered each of these lives, you have the memory of each of them. And then you join the Great Spirit on a higher plane of existence."

"What happens at that point, Agnes?"

"It is different for each person. Some people join their circle as you have joined the Sisterhood of the Shields, and they go on to do work on higher planes. You may work for many things. You may work for the betterment of the planet that you have spent most of your lives on. You may work on other star levels that you and I here have no knowledge of. It really doesn't matter, because how you evolve really depends on where you go."

"So, Agnes, part of what I am doing with Catherine is trying to understand my many lives so that I can sit in the center of my circle."

"Yes, and I will explain much more of that to you later on in this traveling of yours. Is there anything that bothers you now, anything that you are feeling uncomfortable about?" she asked, picking up a piece of grass that lay next to her sage and beginning to chew on it. Her face looked kind and very old as the flames of the fire reflected on the furrows of her dark brown skin. Her hair was pulled back into a single long braid, and she wore a red shirt with a denim jacket over it matching her denim skirt. She wore the beaded shield that she had been wearing ever since I met her. It was red and white and had the symbol of the turtle beaded intricately into the design. The turtle represents our Mother Earth, and I thought how much Agnes represented the power of Mother Earth to me. In a sense she was the source of my power and my happiness.

"Doubling in the Dreamtime," Agnes went on, "is a very tricky matter. What we are doing, Ruby and I, when you are out in that other dimension, is moving along your lifeline to make sure that everything is in order."

"What could possibly happen to it?" I asked, getting a little frightened at the thought. I was thinking in my mind of an air line reaching down to a deep-sea diver that might snap.

As if she read my mind, Agnes started to chuckle. "No, Lynn, nothing is going to happen to you. We wouldn't let it."

"Could anything happen if you were not here?" I asked.

"Not really, because you have come to the point where you know unconsciously when trouble begins. You would snap back into your body as quickly as a rubber band would snap on my finger. But snapping back that way would make you very uncomfortable."

"I see," I said, still not feeling secure.

"You have prepared for this journey for fifteen years. Your work has made you strong. Your spirit is strong, and more than that, Lynn, there are forces protecting you that you don't even know anything about—and it is better that you do not. There will come a day when you will meet these forces, and then you will understand what all of this really means."

"You know, Agnes, I have never delved much into past lives. I have never known quite what I felt about that subject, because I felt maybe my past lives were largely a product of my imagination. I know that the imagination is very important in the work of a shaman, but I still didn't fully trust what I saw. I have had glimpses of lives as a native person somewhere in the world and so forth, but I didn't trust those glimpses."

"For you, Lynn, it is probably better that you do not, but this is something else, don't you agree?" Agnes asked.

A yellow dog that had been hanging around the cabin for several days poked his nose in through the flap, his round, alert eyes asking if it was all right for him to enter. "Come here, boy," Agnes called to him gently. He came over and lay down beside her and rested his head on her knee. She began to stroke him, playing with his ears. The dog went right to sleep, closing his eyes in complete contentment.

"Even though I have been back from that last journey for thirty or forty minutes, Agnes, I'm still very wobbly. I feel that my reactions start to be Catherine's reactions. It's getting difficult to know where my existence begins and hers leaves off."

"I would say that is normal. I think that if it becomes more pronounced, you should tell me. I think that at this moment you don't have anything to worry about. Your luminous fibers that form your spirit being are very strong. I have moved along them like someone walking in space along a lifeline. They are secure and strong, and you are meant to be doing what you are doing. I would never ask you to do it if it were not important; you will learn things through this previous lifetime that are invaluable to you.

"It is also important for the people that you work with to know that this is something that is possible, that this is indeed an exercise that strengthens your spirit. There is nothing you do that does not strengthen your spirit. That is what this life is all about—to evolve. So everything you do is an exercise, in a way. It 'exercises the muscle' in a sense. If you want to become a good horseback rider, you exercise your muscles so that you can become proficient at that endeavor. This work in other lifetimes is important because it enhances your abilities to travel between the dimensions."

"Agnes, in my dreaming with Catherine, Grandmother talks about the ancient knowledge of Europe that she was a part of, the way of Wyrrd. And she talks about where that knowledge came from originally. She talks about the Star Nations that came." I looked up toward the top of the Dreamlodge, trying to remember the number of years. "It was at least three hundred thousand years ago, I think."

Agnes looked at me with a twinkle in her eye and nodded. "Yes," she said, patting the old yellow dog. "The Star Nations brought this extraordinary knowledge onto our planet. It was lost to most people, but it was memorized all over the world by women. Women are the keepers of the ancient knowledge, and we are the keepers of Mother Earth, because we share her energy, because we share her source of power. Because of our connection with Mother Earth it is fitting for women to preserve this knowledge. Down through the ages it has been passed from a woman to her daughter or adopted daughter, her apprentice, and that apprentice then becomes a shaman woman and passes it on, and so forth.

"In a few places at different times this knowledge has been written down. It has always been mixed with other knowledge, but basically it has been kept the same for all time. It is very ancient. Many times the hoops of knowledge have been broken, but never has the knowledge been forgotten. Women have kept it in one way or another. We must do great honor to those women, because many of them have suffered enormous hardship first to learn the knowledge, then to pass it on—all the while trying just to live."

"Agnes, what happened to the Star Nations? Did they come and then just leave?"

"No one knows for sure, my daughter. They came from the stars, and to the stars they returned, but we think they have brought back their knowledge from time to time, that they have manifested this knowledge through people who have walked the earth. These people have known where to find wisdom."

"What do you mean find wisdom?" I asked.

"The Star Nations planted wisdom, like seed pods, upon the earth. We spoke of this in Tibet when we went there together, you remember. These seed pods were meant to bloom and bear fruit when the peoples of the earth were ready for higher knowledge," Agnes said. She looked away, her eyes suddenly very dark and remote.

"Where are these seed pods?" I asked.

"Many have been found by the great teachers that lived, and many are still dormant. They are somewhere in the river waters, hidden in the rocks of the mountains, or within the roots of the trees somewhere in the world. One day they will all be found, and one day this great Mother Earth will be healed by the wise ones who love her." Agnes looked at me, with tears of longing in her eyes, and smiled. "One day we will truly understand. All religions, I believe, speak of a holy man who has come and walked among them and imparted great knowledge to them. That wise being has always come from the Star Nations.

"Some of the animals and the plants have also come from the stars. In the east the Bedouins talk about the Arabian horse and the saluki as having come down from the stars, gifts from Allah. I believe that is true. They are the oldest breeds of horse and dog in the world. And they are indeed different."

Agnes reached over to my altar and took a little bundle of tied herbs and held it up in the firelight.

"Here. These are from the star people."

"What are they, Agnes?" I hadn't noticed them. They looked different from any of my herbs.

"These are nettles, and they are used to keep away the darkness, negativity, the dark spirit that may come to harm you."

"But the dark spirit would not harm me, Agnes, because I won't let it. Who would send me such a thing?"

"You would only send such a thing to yourself," Agnes said with a smile. "You remember your lessons well from Nepal, I hope."

"Yes, Agnes, I do. They were some of the most important lessons I've ever learned. I learned that our fear creates our own negativity. Negativity from other people as a thought form can certainly come into my field, but it's not going to harm me unless I allow it to. I can send it back to the person who sent it to me."

"Yes, this is true, but there are times when we are weak," Agnes said. "There are times when it helps to have our plant friends around us. A dark spirit sees these plants and leaves quickly," Agnes said, putting the bunch of nettles back onto the altar and dusting her hands together.

"Where do those nettles come from?" I asked.

"They come from Zoila in the south in the Yucatán and Guatemala."

"Oh," I said, remembering Zoila and José and Jaguar Woman with fondness. "Agnes, is Grandmother, in my dreaming with Catherine, the woman who chose her death so that I could become part of the Sisterhood?"

Agnes laughed. "I don't know, Lynn. I think that's for her to tell you, and perhaps you can tell me."

"Agnes, I know that you know."

"Well, this might surprise you, but I don't know everything," Agnes said as she got to her feet.

The old yellow dog got up and stretched, first one hind leg straight out behind him, then the other. I got up and put out the fire, and we walked out of the Dreamlodge. We said a prayer outside the lodge, smudged it all the way around, and then walked back up the trail toward Agnes's cabin. It was now dark out. We could see the moon poking through the clouds above, leaving shadows of branches and trees on the smooth ground ahead of us. The old yellow dog seemed quite happy that we were heading toward the cabin and dinnertime. As the cabin came into view, a plume of smoke left the chimney. It smelled of cedar, and my stomach began to growl. I was starving.

As if hearing us, Ruby threw open the door of the cabin. Standing with her hands on her hips, she called to us. "Well, it's about time. We're starving. If you don't leave us physically, Lynn, you leave us in spirit. Aren't we good enough for you?"

"Ruby, I thought you wanted to get rid of me," I laughed.

I went into the cabin and closed the door, and I gasped as I first saw July standing at the kitchen counter. For a moment she looked like my friend Anne in the Dreamtime. My eyes went wide, and my jaw dropped. July slowly turned around with a tray of food she was taking to the table in the center of the room. She stopped and looked me in the eyes. She seemed surprised, but a moment later I thought I saw a knowing behind her gaze. And then she cast her eyes down and placed the tray on the table. I glanced at Agnes, who was looking at me intently. I was suddenly frightened. I don't know what it was—perhaps just the surprise. I looked at Agnes questioningly, but she smiled and shook her head as if I should be quiet, so I said nothing.

"Do you think we could eat tonight without a lot of talk?" Ruby asked.

"Sure, Ruby, but I thought maybe you'd like to hear about my journey."

"You just love to make me envious of all the wonderful places you get to go to. You always leave me at home. No thanks. I think I'd just like to eat in peace for once," Ruby said.

Before July sat down she came and gave me a quick hug around the shoulders. "Lynn, we've missed you. I would love to hear your story." She sat down and looked at me expectantly.

"Not now. I think Lynn needs to eat. She's more tired than she knows," Agnes said.

With those words I suddenly realized how exhausted I was. I felt as if I had run back and forth to Ruby's cabin two or three times. I ate like I had never eaten in my life.

Ruby finally sat back and said, "Well, I hope you're going to leave some for us."

"Don't worry, Ruby. I'll leave you a bite or two."

She pinched me on the cheek with a threatening glare and said, "Yes, I hope you'll leave a bite or two for your old friend Ruby."

My stomach did a quick turn. When Ruby looked at me that way with her blind eyes, I knew something was in the air. I didn't know quite what, but I knew that this was going to be a very long night. I had hoped that I would be able to sleep, but as I finished my dinner, a new surge of energy quickened me, and I wanted to talk. I began looking forward to the adventure of the night with Agnes, Ruby, and July.

"Oh, talk, talk, talk," Ruby said. "All this seriousness — maybe tonight is a night we can play a little game. How about it, Lynn? Are you up for a game?"

I breathed a deep sigh and knew that the butt of this game was probably going to be me. "Okay," I said, "I guess I'm ready for anything."

Ruby chortled to herself. I didn't like the sound of that. July and I got up and cleared the table and washed the dishes. Agnes and Ruby were getting two peculiar-looking objects wrapped in blankets out from under the bed. They set them out on the table. The two bundles looked identical. I had never seen them before.

"Where did those come from?" I asked.

"Never you mind," Ruby said. "We get around once in a while too, you know."

She sat by the table as July stoked the fire. Agnes got herself settled comfortably and indicated she wanted me to come and sit next to her.

"Simon says touch your nose," Agnes said in a loud voice to me.

"Simon says, you must be kidding," I said to everyone; they were all touching their noses.

"You're out," Ruby said, laughing.

"Simon says hop on one leg," Agnes demanded as we all hopped on one leg.

After an hour of giggling and running around the cabin, I realized why we had played this silly game. By concentrating on what was happening, I had pulled my astral and physical body completely together again. Then Agnes unwrapped two masks from the bundles. One was an old Tlingkit spirit mask, which she placed on the back of a chair at the head of my sleeping bag for guidance and strength in my dreamwalking. The other mask was Wolf, and she placed that mask at the foot of my bag to strengthen my power animal and pay her respect. By the time I went to bed, I felt whole and normal, and I rested well.

My next dreaming began early the following morning.

CHAPTER 9

LIVING
IN
LIFE FORCE

It HAD BEEN RAINING and storming for over a week, so I had not been to see Grandmother in all that time. My parents wouldn't let me leave the house. I awoke at dawn on the fourteenth day, threw open my draperies, and looked out at a cloudy sky, but no rain. I was thrilled. I knew that perhaps this afternoon I could go to see her. Finally, after the midday meal I saddled up my horse and left for the little stone house. I had stuffed a big finger of bread in my pocket for her, but by the time I arrived and was standing in her living room, the bread had been squashed and turned to mush. Sheepishly, I emptied my pocket out onto a plate on the table.

Grandmother came over and gave me a big hug. She was very glad to see me. She stoked the fire, made us something hot to drink, and served me some soup. It was still very cold outside and the wind was blustery, but at least there was no rain. She set two chairs in front of the fire so that we could put our feet on pillows and be warm. She took out her embroidery and handed some to me, and we sat in silence, watching the fire and doing our needlework.

After some time she looked at me, her eyes twinkling with light reflected from the flames. "It is good just to be together, is it not, Catherine?"

I studied Grandmother's face for a moment. She seemed to be saying something more than just her words. "Yes, Grandmother, being together is very important to me."

Grandmother worked steadily on her embroidery, pulling a green thread through a white background. After several minutes she said, not looking up, "It is that state of being that I am talking about. It is that being, that silence, that unspoken closeness that nourishes an important part of you. It is something that I want you to learn about."

After several minutes Grandmother knotted the thread, broke it off between her teeth, and set the embroidery in her lap. "Catherine, you are very young. Because of that, you are very innocent. You are as wide open as that pasture out there. Do you know what I mean?"

I sat quietly, running my fingers over the flower designs in my embroidery. I tried to sense inside myself what she was talking about, and I felt the frightened little girl inside me. I looked at Grandmother. "Yes, I think I know what you mean. Right now I sense that innocent part of myself as frightened, as that part of me that does not know how to protect myself."

"I think what protecting yourself really means, particularly at your age,

Catherine, is nourishing that part of you that you think of as 'I,' 'me.' You have difficulty doing that. You give a lot to the world, do you not, to the people around you?" Grandmother asked.

"Yes, I do, but probably not as much as I should be giving."

"There are times, Catherine, when you have to think just about yourself. There are times when it is not a bad thing to be selfish; there are times when it helps you be strong. If you are not strong, if you cannot make your way in the world, then you cannot be an example for other women."

"How do I nourish myself, Grandmother? I am not sure I understand what you mean."

"Rather than tell you, Catherine, I want you to do something. Sit there and look at me. Keep your eyes open, and just look into my eyes. We will sit here for a while. Just do this practice with me, and let us see how you feel."

The fire crackled, almost in response to her words. A cloud passed overhead, and the room darkened slightly. I took a deep breath, as did she, and we just sat in quiet peacefulness looking at each other. It was simple, and it was very silent. At one point Grandmother looked at me very intently and smiled.

"Do not let words get in your way. Just relax and let go," she said.

I took another deep breath, and we sat in silent communion, like two old friends sitting in a garden. At first I felt nervous. I wanted to talk; I was embarrassed; I felt shy. And then my heart began to open, and after many minutes, I was bathed in a feeling of expansive love for this friend of mine, my new friend, who was giving me so much. I felt blessed, and instead of trying to radiate that feeling to her, I sat inside that feeling, and I wrapped a feeling of beingness around me like a cocoon, a soft, luminous egg of comfortable feeling.

After some time Grandmother shifted a bit in her chair. She smiled broadly and winked at me. "There, you see, that was not so bad, now, was it?"

"Well, I don't know, Grandmother. It was a beautiful feeling."

"I want you to understand, Catherine, what that feeling truly is. Do you sense how that feeling nourished the 'I'ness within you, your feeling of self? Do you not feel that you gave a special meal, a special nurturing, to that sense of 'I' within you?"

I considered it for a minute, then nodded my head. "Yes, Grandmother, I really do. I feel nourished, as if I had just eaten a big piece of honey cake. I feel better. Yes, I understand what you are saying."

"My child, when you are feeling lonely at home and you cannot come to see me — if it is raining, or it is storming, or your parents have things for you to do — move into that still place inside yourself, just quietly. There is no mystery. Let your heart open. Let the whole room be filled with nourishing light from your heart. Do you understand, Catherine? Now let us have some buttermilk," she said.

I jumped up and added small branches to the fire, then came back to Grandmother with two cups of buttermilk. We sipped our buttermilk and went on with our needlework.

All of a sudden Grandmother jumped. "Ouch!" she said.

"What happened, Grandmother?"

"Oh, I just pricked my finger with my needle." She held up her finger. There was a drop of blood on the end of it. She cocked her head to one side, sucked the end of her finger, and then touched the point of the needle with a finger of her other hand.

"This needle point is a bringer of truth. Come over here a minute, Catherine. Touch the end of this needle."

I went over to stand next to her and gingerly touched the point of the needle, not wanting to prick myself as well.

She said, "Touch it just hard enough to cause a little bit of pain." I did so.

"Ow," I said as I accidentally pricked myself. Now I too was bleeding. "Now we can be true sisters," I said.

"Well, yes, Catherine, that is not a bad idea. We are now of common blood." She touched her finger to mine and gave me a kiss on the forehead. "But there is something else I want you to learn," she said. "Sit down."

When Grandmother had something to teach me, her demeanor changed considerably. Instead of being soft and sweet and gentle like anybody's grandmother, she became strong and remote. Her eyes shifted from gentleness to intensity. The change always frightened me a bit, but I realized that when she moved into that place of power within herself something important was coming through, and I had to pay attention. I moved back to my chair and sat quietly sucking on my finger.

"Catherine, have you ever been in pain?"

"Oh, yes, Grandmother."

"Can you remember that pain?"

"Well, yes, as a matter of fact, I feel it in my finger right now. This hurts," I said.

"Take the needle," she said. I picked up the needle and held it in front of me. "Now, look at the needle. Look at the point of it; describe it to me."

"Well, it is pointed; it's sharp; it shines in the light; it reminds me of being at the center."

"Good, Catherine. Now, as that needle has a pointedness to it, a centeredness to it somehow, I want you to go inside yourself. Close your eyes." I did as I was told. "Close your eyes, and move your consciousness into your finger."

I did so. It was not hard, because my finger was now throbbing. I moved my consciousness down into my finger, and then she said to me, "I want you to try to feel your life force. Are you pulling it in, or are you pushing it out, or are you just sitting with it?"

I thought for several minutes. "I think I am pulling my life force in. It is as if I want to pull the force away from the hurt."

"Good. Now, Catherine, I want you to do the opposite. I want you to push the life force out through the pain in your finger. Try that for a few minutes."

I did that, and as I did it, I felt the pain throb. I felt the throbbing in my finger. That was all.

"Just sit with the pain," Grandmother said.

I did that. I just sat with it. I did not push the energy in or out.

"Now, Catherine, I want you to tell me where that pain really is."

I took my consciousness and went into the pain—except a strange thing happened. As I moved into the pain, the pain moved off to the left, and then off to the right, and then all of a sudden, it was not there. It was gone. I could not find it. I started shifting in my chair. Grandmother started to laugh that wonderful laugh of hers, and I couldn't help but laugh with her. I opened my eyes.

"What are you laughing at, Grandmother?"

"I am laughing at the look on your face," she said. "Well, where did you find the pain?"

"Grandmother, there is no more pain. I could not find it."

"Ah, is that not interesting? Well, now that the pain is gone, perhaps we can finish our buttermilk."

I looked at her. I could not believe what had just happened. I looked down at my finger. The bleeding had stopped, and I certainly felt no pain.

"But, Grandmother, every time I have ever pricked my finger, it has hurt for hours. My fingers are very sensitive."

"Yes, Catherine," she said with a grin.

"What just happened, Grandmother?"

"You found out something very important."

"What was that?" I asked.

"You found out that pain is very interesting, and perhaps we think it should exist because we have been hurt. But maybe in fact it is only in our minds."

"But Grandmother, if I hurt my leg, if I had a cut, it would hurt terribly. Of course there is pain in the world."

"Yes, there is pain in the world, but let us just say that there are ways to work with pain."

I looked at her for several moments, blinking. Then I remembered, I do not have any pain. "I guess you are right, Grandmother. I do not have any pain. I just did that myself, did I not?"

"Yes, you did."

"Well." I shook my head. It was hard to believe.

"You see, Catherine, these are things that are not easy to explain, because if they are explained to us, we do not believe the words we hear. It is very important to experience these things. You have done it, and you can do it again."

"Yes, Grandmother. Thank you."

The old woman and I sat quietly in front of the fire for some time. My thoughts turned to Anne.

"Grandmother, where is Anne?" I asked.

"She had to go home to be with her family for a while, but she will be back soon. She likes you very much, Catherine. I am so glad that the two of you are friends."

"Oh, Grandmother, so am I. I never thought I would have such a wonderful friend. You have changed my life."

The old woman smiled broadly, her eyes nearly disappearing. She was very pleased. "Yes, Anne is a good girl. She has a very strong self shield."

"Is that different from a spirit shield? When I think of a shield, Grandmother, I think of the shields that warriors carry when they go into battle. My father has many such shields hanging on the walls."

"Well, Catherine, there are outside shields and inside shields. A self shield is your identity in the physical world. A spirit shield is an inside shield. Some shields we carry in the world to protect us. Some have a coat of arms that tells the world who we are. And then there are shields inside, and they protect us also and help us know who we are."

"It is almost as if we have many different people inside us. Is that right?"

"Yes, it is true. There are many different parts to ourselves, and to become a woman of knowledge, a woman of Wyrrd, you must understand the meaning of all parts of yourself. There is a part of you that is actually just your vitality, your life force. That is why I did that earlier exercise with you, that being in the silence with me, because you are getting to know the part of yourself that is just being or just a quality of living in your life force."

"Yes, I do not spend enough time there. I wish I had more time to experience that."

"When you are at home, Catherine, do you spend very much time alone?"

"Yes, I do, but I am always busy. I am always working on my projects, doing my needlework, studying music, or doing whatever my mother wants at the time. And that is my life, I suppose."

"Let me ask you another question, Catherine. Do you enjoy being as busy as you are?"

"Oh, yes, I like being busy. I find that I like to accomplish things very much."

"I see. Is that a part of yourself that you are familiar with?"

"I do not understand what you are asking."

"Well, just as there is a part of you that likes to just be, there is a part of you that likes to do things."

"Oh, yes, I see what you mean, Grandmother. Yes, that is a big part of me."

"Perhaps the part of you that is always accomplishing things has taken over the part that just likes to relax in silence, maybe even to the point where the part of you that likes to just 'be' is overshadowed. Is that possible?"

I thought for some time, squirming in my chair. There was something that felt uncomfortable about what she was asking. "Yes, I think that is true. So what does it mean, Grandmother?"

"The important thing is that you experience the difference between these two parts of yourself, my daughter. But also, it is important for you to understand that there is a choice. You have the choice to do too much or just enough, and you also have the choice just to 'be.'"

"That is true, I am sure, but everybody pushes me, you know. Everybody wants me to be busy all the time."

"As you get older then, Catherine, you can see the error in that. You can remember the nourishment you get from sitting in the center of your own being, and when you begin to feel hungry inside for time, for space, you can take that time, and you will know how to nourish yourself and replenish yourself. Every day the body needs food and it needs sleep. Your spirit is just the same. The spirit shield that we have spoken of needs to be nourished. For there to be flames, for you to arouse the inner fire, there must be something to burn. For there to be power, there must be life force. So it is important for you to see how to nourish yourself, whether I am around or not."

I nodded and realized deep inside me the importance of her words.

"Your spirit shield can become dented at times," Grandmother went on. "It happens when people hurt your feelings, when you face difficulties, when you are frightened, when you move out of that silent place inside you."

"Is there anything I can do?"

"Yes, I will show you."

She stood up and indicated for me to do the same. The room was getting even darker now. The firelight danced across her face, making her look very ancient and very regal. She had an extraordinary presence. She looked like the queen of the world. She was a powerful woman hidden away here in this little stone house in the country. I wondered where she had come from, and for a moment I sensed her extraordinary history and the series of events that had brought her to me. And I wondered at the mystery of our meeting.

"Catherine, extend your arms like this." She held her arms with her palms straight up in front of me. "Now, close your eyes, and feel gently around you. There will be a misty feeling, a feeling almost of a gentle cloud around you. Take a deep breath, and feel this cloud. At first it will be warm, then cool. You will be feeling the light around you. Move your hands around, and you will feel that in front of your heart, your spirit shield has moved very close into your body. In a moment, I want you to move your spirit shield out away from your body about the length of one of these fire logs," she said. She crushed a few herbal leaves into a green mass and smudged my forehead between my eyes. I peeked at the fire log and saw that it was about the length of my arm.

"Now, with your hands, gently, using your imagination, visualize your spirit shield, this golden white light all around you, the color of the flames in the sun, and with your palms push your spirit shield out to arm's length, gently and with intent."

"What do you mean by intent, Grandmother?"

"I mean center your attention around your navel, and then push out with your thoughts, and you will begin to actually feel your spirit shield. Now, begin."

I centered myself, and then I began to push out with my hands. At first I felt nothing. Finally, I could feel a gentle warmth. As I began to push, it became warmer, as if the activity had warmed the light around me. Slowly, I could see. I could sense something burning intensely like a cocoon or a shield of light that enveloped me. Slowly, I pushed it out until I felt more comfortable again. The smudge between my eyebrows tingled slightly.

"Ah," Grandmother said. "That is good. Now we will sit down and just be together for a while, and then I think it will be time for you to go home, Catherine."

I sat down again with Grandmother and looked at her. I smiled. "Grandmother, I feel so much more calm, yet powerful at the same time. Is that a trick?"

"I suppose you could call it a trick, Catherine, but it is as real as the nose on your sweet face. These are just things that we need to know about. People do not learn these things; they are afraid to become wise. Human beings are afraid to try anything new. It is the tragedy of human life, as we have spoken about before. Even though something new may make us feel better, we are still afraid."

"Well, I am not afraid, Grandmother. I do not understand why everyone else is." I picked up the embroidery and began tying off the threads.

"Well, child, you are not afraid because your understanding is much deeper. There will be a time—a long while from now—when the world will be happier and a better place to live. Whether you know it or not at this moment, some of that improvement will be because of the work you are doing now."

I looked at her, hardly able to believe her, not knowing what to say. I sensed that she meant some time long in the future, but I was not sure.

"Do not worry at this moment, Catherine. There are many things you will learn in our work together. Now it is important only that you experience these simple things. But even though they appear to be very simple, you are learning truth that will be valuable for a very long time, certainly longer than you know." She leaned forward and brushed the herbs off my forehead.

I said nothing and finished the knot that I was working on. Then I glanced toward the window and the gathering clouds. Grandmother and I went outside, and she untethered my horse, who whinnied softly as I approached. I gave him an apple and hugged him and petted his neck. He pawed the ground. He know he was going home to dinner. I gave Grandmother a big hug, mounted, and galloped off down the road.

My saddle had a feathered cantle. It was quilted and very comfortable to sit in, and I had never seen another saddle like it. I enjoyed it and took very good care of it. My father had given it to me on my seventh birthday. It had been a little big at the time, but now it fit me perfectly. I felt the strength of my horse underneath me as he cantered happily down the road. I reined him to the side of the lane where the dirt was softer. I looked out to the horizon, streaked now with orange and pink and purple light. For a moment it reminded me of the light that I had seen around Grandmother when I had walked into her house that day. I was filled with a warmth I can only describe as a spirit warmth. I felt loved and happy and more at ease than I ever remembered being. I had a sense that there was an old woman inside me, that even though I was young and looked young, I was also ancient. I felt as old as Grandmother. I did not feel stiff or ill, but I did feel the weight of many years. I wondered about that, and I told myself that I would ask Grandmother about it the next time I met with her.

. . .

I awoke, lying on the sheepskins of the Dreamlodge. A clap of thunder had brought me to consciousness. The entire structure was shaking and squeaking and creaking in the wind. For a moment I was scared. I lay back against the sheepskins, gathering my senses, and remembered where I was. I took a deep breath and relaxed, feeling uneasy. My body hurt all over, and I felt a little sick to my stomach. I wondered how long I had been gone. I looked over to the fire. It had burned down to red coals and was very warm. I did not feel cold on the outside, but there was a coldness inside me, a coldness as if I had been gone from my body for a very long time. I rubbed my arms and legs and took several deep breaths, not really having the strength to get up, not really wanting to. I settled back down into my sheepskins and tried to recall exactly what had happened. I remembered the road that I had just been riding down on my horse. I shook my head. I couldn't really bring myself back into present reality; a part of me was still gone. It was a little frightening.

Agnes came in, parting the blankets hanging over the entrance to the Dreamlodge. She came and sat with me and brought me a blueberry muffin. I sat up, looking at it, and took it in my hands. It was soft and warm, and it smelled good. A tiny cloud of heat was rising from it. I sniffed the steam and took a tiny bite of the muffin. I looked at Agnes and shook my head.

"Yes?" she asked.

"Agnes, I'm having a hard time." I burst into tears. "I feel as though I have one foot in one dimension of time and one foot in another. I feel I'm being pulled apart. Are you sure this is good for me?"

"Yes, Lynn. This is not dangerous for you as long as you do not stay away too long at one time. There is no question that it's hard on your body."

She began to rub my arms as I sniffed a little and stopped weeping. She shook her head. "Your arms are very cold. Your body is very cold, Lynn. I don't want you to be gone so long next time."

"But I don't know how to come back, Agnes. I come back whenever I come back. I think the thunder brought me back."

"What thunder?" Agnes asked.

"Well, the thunder and the wind."

Agnes looked at me strangely. "Why, Lynn, there is no wind outside. It's broad daylight. It's a beautiful sunny day; there's no thunder."

She got up, took the amulet necklace off my neck and replaced it over my altar, and opened up the blankets of the door. I looked out. It was indeed sunny. The leaves on the poplars surrounding the lodge did not even move. There was not a breath of air.

"Well, Agnes, I heard a crack of thunder, and this whole lodge was shaking when I woke up. That's all I know."

"It is just spirit. It is spirit helping you. Spirit has come to protect you. Power wants you to know that it is here."

CHAPTER 10

LANGUAGE
OF THE
PLANTS

Nothing works
quite so violently
as religion turning in the shade
of oaks and pine.

A DAY WENT BY BEFORE my next journey in the Dreamlodge. I slept a lot and washed some clothes in the creek with Agnes, Ruby, and July. By the time I reentered the Dreamlodge, I was rested and felt ready to dreamwalk again. I took the necklace with the amulet from above the altar, placed it around my neck, and lay down.

I entered Catherine's world late in the day. It was afternoon, and we were sitting in Grandmother's house. As I looked up at the window with the sun shining through, a large spiderweb in the corner caught my eye. It had been perfectly executed and shone like spun crystal in the sunlight. I mentioned it to Grandmother. She took my arm and pulled me over to the window.

"Catherine, look very closely. See how intricately designed and built this spiderweb is. Look how it is made out of one continuous thread."

Very gently, Grandmother lifted her finger and touched one end of the spiderweb. It jiggled all over. "See," she said, "if you step on one edge of the web, it makes the rest of the web move accordingly."

I looked at Grandmother, wondering what she was getting at.

"Do you remember when you saw me for the first time with my spirit shield exposed?" she asked me.

"Yes, Grandmother."

"Do you remember seeing some fibers around me?"

I thought for several minutes, still looking at the spiderweb. Then I recalled that I had indeed seen something. I had thought it was part of the flames, but now that she asked me to think about it, I realized it was something else.

"Yes, Grandmother, I saw something. It looked like — well, actually, it looked like a spiderweb in a way. Just very slightly and subtly I saw a web of light around you in and amongst the flames."

"We are built of fibers, my daughter, and between each and every being that is alive is a network of fibers not unlike this spider web. It is important to understand this, because if I move here" — Grandmother did a little jig, lifting her skirt and smiling — "if I do a movement here in my mind, in my emotions, with my energy physically or simply with my spirit shield, in one way or another it affects someone living on the other side of England. Any movement I make produces corresponding movement over there. I am affected, in the same way when that person moves or sends out a positive or negative thought.

"As a woman of Wyrrd, you will begin to learn and understand this. You will begin to feel the tugging on your fibers. If I am thinking about you because I am your teacher, you will feel it. And if I am thinking about you in the middle of the night and you are sound asleep, you will awaken, and you will know that something has happened, that I need you."

"Will I really be able to feel those things from you? If I send you a thought, Grandmother, will you receive it?"

"Yes, Catherine, that is one of the lessons of the power of Wyrrd that you must learn. You must learn to master this."

She moved over to a beautiful tapestry of knots that was hanging on the wall. I had always been fascinated with it; it was unlike anything I had ever seen. "Come and look. Your fibers are not unlike this tapestry."

"Where did it come from?" I asked.

"It came from a place that I was in a long time ago, a place I told you about, Catherine. It came from my teacher in the ancient world of Wyrrd. It has a very important meaning to you and to all women and men who study the way of Wyrrd. I want you to look at the way these knots are tied. I want you to see how the fibers are interrelated."

I walked over to the tapestry and ran my fingers over the smooth surface.

"Look up in the corner, Catherine."

I looked up in the corner and saw that actually the tapestry was made of one long piece of thread. I traced my fingers along the silken thread and realized that someone had knotted it in such a way that it made an entire beautifully designed tapestry.

"How is this possible, Grandmother?"

"It is possible only for a magician. You or I could not sit here with a long piece of thread and make anything out of it but a snarl."

She smiled to see me still awe-struck, my eyes wandering over the tapestry from beginning to end.

"You as a self shield are a continuous cord, but your fibers are too tightly knit in their weaving. Somewhere in your history, you have learned these power things before, perhaps. Because of that, you can see the lights around me. Because of that, your learning is not as arduous as it might be for someone else. But we need to loosen those fibers in your personal weave even more."

"What do you mean by loosening my fibers?" I asked. I felt my arm and placed my hand over my stomach. "I feel very firm to myself."

Grandmother laughed at me and poked her finger into my ribs, which made me jump.

"Let us go back to the spiderweb."

We looked again at the intricate spiderweb, which was now turning a beautiful rose color in the light of the setting sun.

"You see, this spider has woven up all the corners of existence, in a sense," Grandmother said with a faraway look in her eyes. "There was a great magician once. We called her simply the Weaver. She knew how to pull together the energies of the universe into one place."

"But how is that possible, Grandmother?"

"She understood how the fibers work. She knew that they were luminous and that they could be manipulated."

"But how? Do you mean you can take your hand and start pulling on a fiber?"

"Well, in a way you can. Again, this is part of the unknowable. It is part of the world of Wyrrd that you are learning about. Some people are very talented at working with the fibers. The magician who made that extraordinary tapestry was one of them."

"Is she still alive, Grandmother?"

"You could say that she is."

"I do not understand, Grandmother."

"That is a subject we will talk about later. I think it is best left alone for now. But I want you to look again at the spiderweb. The spiderweb is very small. It is made by the spider to catch its food. In a sense that is what you do with the fibers within you. You begin to understand as we work that there are things and situations and people that you need in your life, and you can bring them to you. But you do that by making a place within yourself for them to live."

I still did not understand.

"Let us say that you wanted to marry a certain young man. If that were true, then inside of you you would make yourself available for him. Is that not correct?"

"Yes, I think so."

"It is the same way with power. If you want power, you have to make a place inside you for power to live. In the way of Wyrrd there is something that we call the jewel or the diamond. The word is hard to translate, because it is not something physical. And in fact it is something that cannot really be explained. But I can tell you how you need to be for that diamond to reside within you. First, you need to be receptive. Second, you need to be very strongly centered in your energy right here at your navel."

Grandmother reached out and pressed my stomach around the navel area.

"When we sit in a state of beingness together, you are beginning to touch the edges, the perimeter, of that diamond. You are beginning to stroke your consciousness over the face of one facet of that diamond. When you can finally stretch your consciousness around that diamond to enfold it, you will be a very, very powerful woman."

"Do you have a diamond, Grandmother, inside you?"

"Yes, my daughter, I do. My teacher taught me how to make a home for that jewel many long years ago, and that is why I have been able to withstand the aloneness that my kind of power creates. There are very few men or women who will ever know who I truly am. Therefore, when I am loved, I am never sure for what reason I am loved. I am never sure that I am loved for who I really am, because no one can really know me."

Grandmother looked out the window. I had never seen a more wistful look on her face. It was not sadness. It was simply a moment of remoteness, a moment when I realized that indeed we were separate. Grandmother looked back at me and pinched my cheek tenderly. "We are friends. Perhaps one day we will know each other in the depth of our being."

"I would be very proud if that could happen," I said. She returned my smile.

"Good. Then let us do some sewing," she said.

We sat down to work on her embroidery. I had a lot to think about. After a time I looked at the old woman and said, "Grandmother, tell me more about the jewel."

Grandmother looked thoughtful. "It is hard to talk about, because the jewel is unnameable really. All I can say is, it is the impenetrable place within you. It is like the center of a hurricane. When you look out at the world, and you see the activity of all human beings, when you see their movement, their spiritual and physical activity, you realize that at the center of all that pandemonium there is a still point, and the still point is within the magician. The still point is the point of creation, the place where true power lives."

Grandmother drew a circle with her finger on the table, and then she pressed a point in the center of that circle.

"You stand here in the center of your being. This point marks the essence of who you are. When you become powerful in life, you stand at the center of your own will and your own intent. There is no one who can move you. You become the immovable one. You become the one who is never outside her power no matter what happens on a physical or a spiritual plane."

"But no one could stand in that power endlessly," I said.

"No one can be a magician every hour of the day," Grandmother said. "But your vision of life will be different once you have visited your homeland, and your homeland is the jewel. Once you have visited that place, you can never really leave it. Perhaps you will become angry at something. Perhaps your feelings will be hurt. But it will not last for long, and most of you might leave the jewel, but never all of you — not once you have entered that domain."

"When someone becomes part of the world of Wyrrd, is that what they are looking for, Grandmother?"

"Yes, they are looking for power. Do you understand why, Catherine?"

"I am not sure, Grandmother."

"I will tell you," the old woman said, looking up from her embroidery. "It is important to understand the value of realizing your dreams in life. But the world of Wyrrd gives you much, much more than just your ability to manifest what you need and want in this lifetime. And remember that this is done without manipulating or hurting anyone around you. It is a healing path, and it is a path of love. But it is also a magical path, and for magic to happen in your life, you must believe in magic."

"But I do, Grandmother. I do believe in magic."

"Well then, my daughter," she said smiling, "you are halfway there. When you look at a spider web and somewhere inside you your fibers resonate with the fibers of that web, you begin to experience the reality of magic. One day you will meet the sisters of Wyrrd."

"Who are they?"

"They are beings of light who live in the world of Wyrrd in another dimension."

"What are you saying? Do you mean they are dead?"

"Not exactly, my daughter. I mean that they are part of the spirit world, and one day soon we will have a spirit circle, and you will learn about these great sisters. They are very powerful, and they are very frightening. When the sisters of Wyrrd come to meet with you, it is the very fact that they frighten you that they can heal you."

"How can that be possible?"

"They see your fear. They see the fabric and the design of the webs within you, and they move into that energy field, and they loosen the fibers. To do that, they must work within your own fear. It is your fear— for once—that can help you."

"And will they help me find the jewel?"

"In a sense they will, because when your web becomes more evenly woven within you, when the cords of life can be manipulated more easily, you will be that much closer to finding that diamond that is surely waiting for its home within you."

"It sounds to me, Grandmother, as if all these things are interrelated."

"Yes." She nodded her head. "That is what I was hoping you would see. It is like that spiderweb over there shining in the sunset light. It is perfection in its design, because it is balanced. That is what you are to become—a perfection of balance. But if you do not come to understand that everything is related to every other thing that you learn in life, you will not be able to accumulate the power that is needed to experience the diamond of Wyrrd."

"In other words, Grandmother, each little thing that you teach me makes me stronger and takes me further along the path."

"That is correct, Catherine. You are a good apprentice, and I appreciate any question that you ask of me."

"Do I have to go someplace to meet the sisters of Wyrrd?" I asked.

"No. No one understands the ways of Wyrrd, but I do know you have made a bid for power in your life. You are sensitive to the elements. You are beginning to understand that we are—you and I and all people, all beings that are alive on this earth—standing on an enormous tapestry called life, and that tapestry is made of fibers. They are luminous and on some level they shine like the sun. You are beginning to walk differently. You are beginning to see the spirit shields, and you are beginning to understand a little about life force. All these things, one and another, are part of each other."

I was fascinated with these new ideas and by the thought of the sisters of Wyrrd.

"Do you mean that the sisters of Wyrrd might visit me at my home?" I asked.

"They may visit you anywhere at any time. You keep looking for them, but they will send you a calling card long before they appear. You will hear a sound that is unmistakable; anyone who belongs to the world of Wyrrd knows the language and the song of the sisters of Wyrrd."

"What does it sound like?" I asked excitedly, a little frightened.

"It is a sound like no other," Grandmother said. She thought for several minutes, cocking her head to one side and absently scratching her forehead.

"I guess you could say that it is a droning sound. Some say that it sounds like the droning of bees or wasps around a nest, but I don't really agree," Grandmother said, shaking her head. "It is more like the droning sound of a million wings."

I looked at her, my eyes wide. "You mean like thousands of birds flying somewhere?" I asked, a little unsure what she meant.

"Yes, something like that, and of course, the sisters appear and sound differently to everyone."

"Well, how do they appear to you, Grandmother?"

"The sound I heard was the staccato note of hooves beating on a hard-packed trail like a thousand horses coming down upon me. I was in a forest, and I was very, very young, and it frightened me almost to death."

Now I really was scared. I looked at Grandmother, not knowing what to make of what she had just told me. "Did they hurt you?" I finally asked.

"You might say that they tore me to pieces, but that is not really true, for I was not physically harmed, exactly."

"What do you mean 'exactly,' Grandmother?" I was not sure I wanted this to happen to me.

"I was bruised afterward, but I never felt any pain. However, they do leave their mark on you. Somewhere on your body you will be bruised, or you might have a rash, or you might have a rubbed place. But it does not hurt. There are a few things you need to learn before this happens."

"What do I need to learn, Grandmother?"

"You need to learn the language of the plant kingdom. You need to learn what plant is yours and what plant will come to your aid if you need her. We will work in the garden late tonight. I am glad that you can spend the night with me," Grandmother said.

"Yes, my family, as usual, I think," I said, laughing a little, "was eager to get rid of me. But why are we going to work in the garden at night?"

"Because there are a few plants that bloom at night — I want you to see them. They are important to your work with the sisters of Wyrrd, and they will protect you."

"Is that why you have all these bundles of herbs?"

"Yes, partly, I would say," Grandmother said, looking around at her bundles of herbs hanging from every nook and cranny in her little stone house.

"Do you use these herbs to heal people?" I asked.

"Yes." She nodded. "From time to time if people need help, they come to me. But as you know, Catherine, I do this very quietly. I do this only for my family and people who know me very, very well. We live in dangerous times, and we must be very clever and very wise about what we do. As you know, our relationship is secret so that this knowledge can be protected and passed down through the ages.

"Come now, Catherine, out into the garden and sit with the plants. Just sit in silence with them. Talk to them, and let them speak to you. The flowers that have a fragrance are asking you to notice them. They are more highly evolved than the blooms without it. The scent brings you to them and enables them to evolve and become more like you, more human. That is the purpose of fragrance. The rose is highly evolved, because it has such magnificent form, as well as a heady scent. They are asking for your love, and they need your light.

"Sit quietly until I call you. I will prepare a meal for us, and then we will sleep for a short time."

I went outside, closed the door to Grandmother's stone house behind me, and found a patch of clover. There I spread a small blanket down on the ground and sat with the plants. Grandmother's garden was very beautiful. It was a tangle of roses and other beautiful flowers of every description, blue and pink and yellow. All were very fragrant, especially the roses and lilacs. Sitting among them was a joy. Every once in a while I would catch a whiff of something unusual, and I would try to follow that scent. At one point there was a very sweet, gentle fragrance coming from over to the left. I walked over and found a beautiful yellow flower on a kind of scraggly bush. I thought this must be something like Scotch broom, but I was not sure. It was delicate and very fragrant. I touched the petals with my fingers. They were soft and velvety and a little damp to my touch. I traced my fingers along the stem, which was very rough and prickly. I was careful not to prick my finger. I went back over to my blanket and closed my eyes. I was completely comfortable and warm as the setting sun bathed my face.

I felt that I had been sitting there only a few minutes when I heard Grandmother's voice calling me to dinner. I opened my eyes, astonished to find myself sitting in darkness. I wondered how long I had been there. I did not feel cold, even though the air around me was quite cold. I pulled my shawl about my shoulders and walked back into the little stone house.

Grandmother had lit several lanterns and set candles on the table. We had a simple meal of stew and bread, which I ate ravenously. We hardly spoke. The fire crackled, and I began feeling very sleepy. Grandmother took me into the bedchamber that I shared with Anne. She pulled down the quilt and set out my things.

"Sleep well, my child, I will get you up in a few hours."

I stripped off my clothes, put on my nightdress, and crawled into bed; I must have been asleep in minutes. Sometime in the middle of the night Grandmother shook me gently. Startled, I looked up into her face. Her lips were smiling; her eyes were intense. I knew that she meant business — this was work time. I got up quickly, threw on my clothes, and drank the cup of warm milk that she handed me.

"It is time, my daughter. The moon is just right. Come with me now out into the garden," she said as she handed me my cape. But we did not stop in the garden as I expected.

"Follow me," Grandmother said, holding up a small lantern so we could see.

We walked on the path through the garden and out the back gate in the dry stone wall, out across a small field, and into Geddington's forest. An owl hooted ominously in a tree high above us. Another owl called back. I was glad that I was with Grandmother. I had never in my life been out in the forest at night. I wondered about all the stories that I had heard about Geddington's forest being haunted and about the elves and the faeries that dwelled at night around the sacred groves of trees. I grabbed hold of the old woman's cloak.

"Grandmother," I whispered, "do not lose me."

Grandmother stopped a moment, and holding up a lantern, looked into my face. "There is nothing to be afraid of, my daughter. Danu and her faeries are with us tonight."

Grandmother's face looked like a gargoyle as the play of lantern flame crossed her furrowed skin. Her eyes were intense and piercing and seemed to look through me. I realized that I had to be very strong and in my power. She was demanding that of me, and I did not want to let her down, even though I was frightened. I couldn't imagine what we were up to. Grandmother thrust a stick into my hand.

"What am I to do with this?" I asked.

"You do as I do," she said.

She turned her back to me and walked briskly down the path, which was partially obscured by a low fog. I stumbled on one stone after another. Before long we came upon a moonlit clearing. The mist lay nestled under the alder trees. The clover glistened in the silvery glow, covered with hoarfrost. We circled the clearing as the old woman sang softly to the faeries and left them food as she searched for various herbs. Then we walked toward a dense grove of oaks.

CHAPTER·11

PLANTS
OF
POWER

W<small>E WALKED A LONG</small> way into the heart of Geddington's forest. My eyes became used to the darkness, and I could see almost
without the lantern. For a long time we searched spaces among the trees
and clearings of clover for plants called lion's paw or lion's foot. I was not
familiar with this plant that Grandmother was looking for, so I watched
her carefully as she picked her way through one bush after another very
tenderly touching the leaves, caressing the branches, talking to the plants
as if they were children or elders, depending on what plants she found.

At one point, as we stood in a pool of moonlight, I looked at the stick
that I was holding and realized it was not an ordinary stick; it had carvings
on it, carvings of runes that were very angular. The symbols were unknown to me. I ran my finger along the grooves and reminded myself to
ask Grandmother about them later; she seemed very intent on what she
was doing and looked as if she did not want me to ask her any questions.

A few minutes later, as if in answer to my thoughts, she pointed with
her stick, which was also carved with runes, and indicated mine. "Catherine, that stick is very, very old, and it is specifically made for digging up
plants."

"At home I have always used a knife to cut plants and to trim them."

"Never, never use metal on sacred herbs — or on any plant — because it
injures the plant and renders it useless for healing purposes. That is why
I gave you a wooden stick, a rune stick that has been used for this purpose
for a very long time. The spirit of the plants is with that stick. Handle it
with care."

I looked down at it with renewed respect.

"Remember, Catherine, never use metal to cut plants or to dig them
up, particularly medicinal herbs, because it will ruin their power."

As we moved through the forest now, we moved from one patch of
moonlight to another, searching through the plants until finally she found
what she wanted. There was a large group of fifteen or sixteen plants —
she called it a tribe — short plants with long green leaves and bristly sur-
faces. The leaves looked, at a certain angle, almost like the paws of a cat.
She motioned for me to come over and kneel beside her. She held her
hands over the plants as if she were feeling something in the air.

"Hold your hands as I do," she instructed. I held my hands with my
fingers apart over the plants. "Now," she said, "close your fingers to hold
your power."

I did as I was told, and instantly I felt a subtle difference. At first I
could feel a coldness. Then she pushed my hands down an inch closer to
the plants, and I began to feel vitality, a subtle heat. She began to sing

over the plants very quietly and to sway back and forth. I closed my eyes and hummed along with her. Soon I felt a sort of wordless communion with the plants. I heard nothing, but I had a sense of strength, a sense of moving closer to the void, as the old woman had called it, a sense of emptiness, of a place of receptivity inside myself.

Grandmother took one of the leaves off the plant and rubbed it between the palms of her hands, producing a pungent smell. She let me sniff it, then she rubbed the back of my neck with the juice from the plant. My neck felt warm, then tingly. It was a young plant, she said.

"This plant is very good for healing muscle stiffness. Now, Catherine, help me dig up these five plants. They are of differing ages, and it will not injure the tribe if we take them away."

She began to dig with her stick, and I did the same. I jabbed the stick down into the ground.

"Catherine, be careful!"

The old woman leaned over, and with great care she pulled the plant I was working on out of the ground, using her digging stick so as not to injure the roots. As she held it up to the lantern light, I could see a gash in the root where I had struck it with my stick.

"Do you see what you have done, Catherine? You have injured the root."

"But Grandmother, I have always just cut plants off at the root when I dig them up in my mother's garden."

"Well, it is the last time you will do that," Grandmother said. "You have injured this plant, and there is nothing we can do about it."

I felt very bad. It was the first time I had ever been reprimanded by Grandmother. Tears stung the back of my eyelids, but I kept on working. Very carefully now, I took the remaining four plants out of the ground. I shook the dirt off their roots, wrapped them carefully in cheesecloth, and placed them in her purple velvet knapsack.

"You did a good job, Catherine. Do not be sad. Everything will be fine now."

I looked into the old woman's eyes. "How did you know which of the plants to dig up?" I asked.

The fire from the lantern made her face look furrowed and rough, not unlike the bark of the king oak nearby.

"You learn to listen to the language of the plants," the old woman finally said.

"You mean they actually speak to you?" I asked.

"Yes, in a way they do. They speak to me with warmth or with coldness. I pick the warm ones, the ones who have more power and have been growing long enough to give me what I need. You can always test power

by the heat—and, in some instances, the cold, but for now we are working with heat. Let me show you."

Grandmother kneeled down again and placed her hands over the
plants. She took several minutes, moving her hands in a circular fashion
with her fingers extended. She seemed not to choose any specific plant.
She put her hands back in her lap and looked at me with a smile.

"Now, Catherine, you do as I just did. This time close your eyes and
bring your spirit shield in toward your navel area. Take a deep breath, and
relax. That's right. Now extend your hands over the plants just as I did.
Take your time, and let the plants speak to you. When they talk to you,
you will feel the warmth. I believe you know enough to do this now."

A cloud moved above us, allowing a bar of moonlight to strike the
clearing and bathe us in a pale and eerie light. The plants were outlined in
a silvery fringe and sparkled under my hands. It took me a long time. I
kept circling my hands very slowly, but as I became more relaxed, I began
to hear a gentle humming sound—very subtle, almost like the sound you
hear in your head when you close your ears with your fingers. Then all of
a sudden I felt a plant underneath my right hand become very warm. I
circled it again and again with my right hand, and then I circled it with
my left hand. I became positive that this plant was speaking to me. It became warmer and warmer. Finally, I stopped, placed my hands in my lap,
and looked at Grandmother, who was now smiling proudly.

"See? I told you you could do it!" the old woman said, poking me in
the ribs. "Tell me what happened."

"Well, at first I felt nothing, and then I began to hear a sound in my
head."

Grandmother seemed quite interested in that. Her face became serious for a moment.

"What exactly did you hear?" she asked.

"A humming sound." I put my fingers in my ears. "It is rather like the
sound you get in your head when you close your ears," I said.

Grandmother reached over and pinched my cheek. "You will be meeting with the sisters of Wyrrd very soon, I suspect. They have given you a
calling card. They love the plants, you know. The plants are their allies.
One of the reasons that I wanted to come and gather from this particular
tribe of plants is because the sisters of Wyrrd also like them very much."

There was an odd light in Grandmother's eyes that made me uneasy. I
looked away, back down at the plant.

"Now show me. Point out to me the plant that spoke to you," Grandmother said.

I pointed to a plant that was a little larger than the others and set off a
little way. The old woman nodded.

"Now I will ask you something else," she said. "Can you tell if that plant is male or female?"

I really did not have the faintest idea, but after I thought for several moments something inside me made me answer female.

"Yes, you are correct. Now, my child, can you tell me whether she is a grandmother or a young one?"

I looked again at the plant. She was bigger than the others, so I immediately said, "Oh, she is a grandmother. Look how tall she is!"

The old woman shook her head, and she said, "You must learn to choose your words more carefully. If you had thought about it, you would realize that all these plants are young ones. Those are the older plants over there." I looked around and saw a stand of much larger plants.

"Are those lion's paws?"

"Oh, yes."

When I looked at them a little more carefully, I realized my mistake.

"Thank you, Grandmother."

"You have learned something tonight. Never think that what is seemingly a simple lesson is really as simple as it looks. Most people in the world, in all of England, could never have done what you have just done tonight. As far as they are concerned, the plants do not have any spirit and could never have spoken to you, nor is one plant colder or warmer than another. You have been able to perceive quite easily what it takes many people years and years to learn. I am very proud of you, my daughter. And now it is time to go home."

CHAPTER · 12

FIBERS
OF
POWER

Settle for less
and you get only what is nearby.
Settle for more
and you receive the complete distance,
the beauty of everything fading.

I LAY ON THE GROUND naked except for the green-dyed cheesecloth that wrapped my body from head to toe. The delicate material covered even my eyes, but I could hear the shriek of a falcon circling high above me. It was night. There was a fire burning nearby, the flames leaping into the sky like wild dancers. Anne held my feet in her lap, and my head rested in the old woman's lap. Grandmother had mixed a paste of some very strong smelling herbs, and she was rubbing it over my forehead and on my cheeks over the webbing of cheesecloth. I was in a deep state of meditation with Grandmother. We had been preparing all day for this ritual. I had not eaten, nor had we talked for many hours.

Now the old woman began to speak in a faraway voice. "Imagine your body completely disappearing. Imagine that your body consists of radiant fibers that shine like the moon — green, luminous fibers of a fabric, tightly woven, that makes up the form of your body. Catherine, take your thoughts into your feet, and visualize the form of your feet, your toes, your heels, your ankles, and your lower legs completely encased in green fabric, very tightly woven. Visualize the threads all the way up the trunk of your body. Do not forget your back and your front and the sides of yourself. See the fabric forming your body all the way up your chest, your arms and hands, and your neck and shoulders, and your whole head completely encased in fabric. Feel the fibers very tightly knit so that if you were to hold it up to the light, the light would not shine through, a very fine and tightly knit fabric like the threads on the dresses that you wear.

"Then move your thoughts inside this newly created form, and imagine your spirit. Imagine your spirit as pink, vibrant light filling the form of green fabric. It is contained and held within. Get a good feeling of what it is like to have your spirit so completely contained and limited. When you have the idea that you want to be invisible, you want not to be vulnerable, you want to be anonymous in the world, this is how you are. You are tightly knit in your physical shield, and your spirit shield, which is the pink light, is limited to the boundaries of the radiant fibers. Take many deep breaths, and stay within your imagining.

"Now, let us try an experiment. Move your thoughts down into your feet. Begin to loosen the fibers. Stretch the fabric with your spirit fingers. Then begin to see little spaces of pink light, little spaces between the threads. Move up your feet, loosening the threads, all the way up your legs, up the trunk of your body, your chest, up your fingers and arms, all the way up to the top of your head. Take your time doing this. This will be a new feeling for you.

"Now, still contain the pink light within those loosened fibers. Then with the force of your will emanating from around your navel area, beginning with your feet, begin to move that pink spirit light out through the spaces between the fibers, out to about two or three inches around your body. Let your spirit fringe out beyond the limits of your form in a soft glow, all the way up your body to the top of your head, so that you will begin to look like a luminous egg of pink light. You will have a feeling, perhaps, of moving into the void, of floating into the abyss, as if you are suddenly more vulnerable than you have ever been in your life. But remember something, Catherine, if you should fall in love someday, and if you contain your light behind those tight fibers, and if you do not know how to let that light move out past your form, you will never truly merge with another human being.

"Take many deep breaths. Now allow that light to begin to move. Sense your breathing. Breathe in and then out. And then sense the beat of your heart, and begin to let that light, your spirit shield, pulsate with your breathing, with the beat of your heart. Do this for several minutes until you feel the full extent of what is happening to you.

"Begin to contract your spirit shield. Bring it back within the boundaries of your form, starting with your feet and moving back up to the top of your head. Bring your spirit shield in, and feel its intensity; feel the constriction and the energy that it takes to hold your spirit shield in such a way. Now take your consciousness back down to your feet, and begin to close up your fibers, from the bottoms of your feet to the top of your head. Close them up tight again.

"Now that you have done that, move yourself into the pink light of your spirit shield, and contract even the light until it becomes a ball of glowing luminosity around your navel. Bring that tiny ball of light down to a pinpoint. Do not let the light disappear completely; make it only a pinpoint of light. Sit with that feeling for a while. Feel how constricted and anonymous you feel. When a dark wizard wants to disappear, wants to be invisible, so he can do his dirty work, this is what he does. He contracts his light and love and makes his fibers impervious to anyone, and he indeed does become invisible, just as you will learn to do. And many other people as well live their lives with their spirit shield only a pinpoint of light hidden inside them.

"Take several deep breaths, Catherine. Let your light expand again inside your fibers. Let it expand and fill you with brightness. Something else is important to understand. Your radiant fibers are shining only because of the light of your spirit. It is like that spider web that we saw in the corner of the window. It begins to look like strands of crystal light only when the sun hits it. It is just the same with your fibers. When they reflect the light of your spirit shield, they become luminous. The more powerful you are, the more radiant your fibers become."

This experience with Grandmother made me feel different than I had ever felt before. I felt as if I had truly gone into the void for the first time. The vulnerability and lack of control I experienced when my spirit body was outside my physical form frightened and excited me at the same time. I wanted the fibers to be loosened, yet I was afraid of the consequences. I was afraid of being too visible in the world.

The paste that had been rubbed on my forehead made me feel very strange. I got sleepy, and then I began to see colors and feel very odd. Again I heard the shriek of the falcon and the sound of his strong wings beating the air as he came closer and closer. I could feel him and hear him circling above me. Then, with a sudden rush of wind from his flapping wings, he landed on the ground next to me. He began picking at the threads of my fibers.

"Do not be afraid. The falcon will not hurt you. He will only loosen your fibers."

I began to hear an extraordinary hum in my ears like the hum I had heard when I was digging the lion's paw. And then I heard more wings. I heard the flapping of huge wings circling above me, the screeches of what I imagined to be a hundred falcons. I could feel the wind created by their wings, and I was in awe and terror of the cacophony of sound. I dared not move. Anne and Grandmother laid their hands on the sides of my body to reassure me. I knew that they would not let anyone hurt me, yet I was still frightened. I could feel the birds diving over my body as if they were looking for their evening meal. Every once in a while a wing would graze the cheesecloth and make my entire body shrink with fear. I could not imagine what was happening. I had never heard so many birds in my life. My mind kept forming strange images of giant eagles and hawks and owls and falcons. For moments at a time, I would pass out then awaken again with strange, horrible monsters in my mind. I could not imagine why it was so difficult to keep awake. I felt the falcon tearing at the threads around my navel area and another falcon tearing at the threads around my knees. I started to scream, but Grandmother held her hand over my mouth. I thought surely these birds would tear the flesh from my bones.

Suddenly, in my mind's eye, I saw a woman's face. She was an old, withered crone, with long, knotted white hair, who was shrieking like the birds with her mouth agape and her eyes wide open and red. She brandished a sword in my direction as if to cut me to pieces. Then her face began to fade off into the light behind her, and a beautiful young face merged with hers. It was smiling and gentle and sweet. She reached out her hands to me.

"Come," she said. "Come and join me. Let me hold you."

I felt my spirit wanting to move toward her. I tried to move my spirit out of my form, but I felt a tremendous ache all over my body, as if I had been thrown from my horse into a pile of rocks.

That was the last thing I remembered. I awoke in Grandmother's house, lying on a pile of rugs and blankets in front of the fire. The old woman was laying a warm cloth over my forehead, and Anne was rubbing my feet, smiling reassuringly. I gasped as I looked up into the face of the old woman. For a moment I thought she might be the woman I had seen in my dream. She too was smiling at me.

"You saw them," she said.

"Who?" I asked, shaking my head and still wondering if I was alive or dead.

"You saw the sisters, did you not?" she asked.

"I saw two very strange women," I said.

"One was old and one young and beautiful?" Anne asked.

"Yes! How did you know?"

"You met the sisters of Wyrrd. You made a bid for power," Grandmother said, "And they have come to you. They have helped you. They have helped to loosen the fibers of your form. Your fibers now will have more luminosity, and you will be able to move your spirit in and out at will."

"They may have helped loosen my fibers, Grandmother, but I do not ever want to see them again. I have never been so frightened in all my life. And what were all those birds doing? I thought they were going to tear me to pieces and have me for dinner." After a moment I calmed down and asked, "Why was one woman old and ugly and one beautiful?"

"The old crone is the dark side of yourself. She is part of what you deny. In her horribleness are many seeds of knowledge if only you can learn to look directly into her eyes and let her teach you. The fair one is also a reflection of you. She represents the beauty of your spirit in life. Now tell me exactly what happened, my child. Here, have a drink of milk."

She lifted my head and helped me sip some warm milk. It made me feel better—I had begun to feel very sick to my stomach. Together, Anne and Grandmother walked me in to my bed. I lay down and began to talk. I could hardly wait to tell them of my adventure. I touched my body all over, wondering what had happened to the green cheesecloth that had wrapped me so tightly.

"It was all part of a waking dream," Grandmother said in answer to my unasked question. "You will be fine now. Just tell me what happened."

Late into the night I talked, telling them the story of my dreaming.

Grandmother interpreted what had happened to me. She told me that I had met the sisters of Wyrrd, and she told me that now I would be able to do my next work with her with much greater ease. She said that I would feel bruised for many days but assured me I would be healthy and stronger for my ordeal.

CHAPTER · 13

SPIRIT
FLIGHT

AT HOME THAT NIGHT I lay in my bedchamber thinking about Grandmother, who had become like a member of my own family, closer to me than anyone I had ever known. She had sent me home to work on seeing my spirit shield and my fibers and seeing the pink light of my spirit shield moving out beyond the boundaries of my body two or three inches. She told me to strengthen my powers of imagery each night before I went to sleep.

For several nights I practiced, just letting the spirit shield move beyond my luminous fibers and then bringing it back ten or fifteen minutes later. Grandmother had told me explicitly what to do once I became comfortable with that. I should not eat too much for dinner (nothing, preferably), go to bed, go into a very silent place, and create a spirit circle in my mind. I was to sit in the center of that spirit circle and begin to loosen my fibers so that the spaces between the fibers were as big as the holes in my loosely knitted shawl.

It was a quiet night — only a gentle wind outside occasionally brushing the trees against the stone walls. I went deeper than usual. I was awake, but in a very, very deep meditative state. I became the fibers of my body, my fibers of power. It was as if I were actually being pried open, separating thread by thread until the pink light of my spirit shield shone like the sun between the fibers.

Instead of feeling vulnerable this time, I felt a sense of, perhaps even a need for, freedom from this physical form. I felt the way a bird would feel with its feet tied to the ground. Grandmother had told me that I might feel a need to fly. She had told me that it would be better for my body if my spirit shield left through the top of my head. She told me to help the spirit shield to do that, to visualize the fibers opening at the crown of my skull. I concentrated with such intensity that I suddenly began to shake. There was a cracking sound at the back of my neck. Suddenly my consciousness was up on the ceiling looking down at my body. I was in my spirit shield, and I was moving around the rafters. I examined them carefully to be sure that I was not fooling myself.

There was a medallion in the center of my ceiling highlighted with gold. I looked at it very carefully and examined the gold leaf that had been applied there many long years ago. It was aged, and there was a thin layer of cobwebs over the entire area.

I felt — as I never had felt in my life before — as if I could fly away from the loneliness and difficulty of my physical existence. Then I had a moment of terror: I wondered if I could find my way back. At that exact moment I dropped back into my body — hard — and it hurt. Suddenly I felt nauseated. My body felt very cold, even though I had been gone only a few minutes. I did not want to be there, so I slipped back out of my body again up through the top of my head. I felt that I wanted to go out through the side of my body toward the ribs, but I remembered Grandmother's warning and did not allow that to happen. I went out through the top of my head and back up to the ceiling again.

This time I tried to relax and enjoy myself, but I realized somehow that my body could not take very much of this, that it was tired, that it needed the spirit shield to come back. I went back into my form, and this time I fell into a very long sleep. I did not wake until the following morning long after I would normally have been at breakfast.

Later that day I went to Grandmother's cottage. She had made some cake, and we sat together nibbling on it and laughing together. I told her excitedly about what had happened to me. She asked me to describe very carefully how I had felt. I told her that I had felt like a bird that wanted to fly and for the first time had found my wings.

"The sisters of Wyrrd are giving you much power, Catherine." The old woman looked at me, seeming very pleased.

"How can I use this power, Grandmother? I know that I am just beginning to understand spirit flight, but what does that power give one in life? How can I use spirit flight to help others, to help myself?"

Grandmother got up and stoked the fire then sat down again at the table, her cheeks rosy red from the warmth of the flames. "Spirit flight is important, Catherine, because it is one more ability. It is like becoming a fine horsewoman. Not only do you learn to ride, but you learn the care of the horse. You learn how saddles are made. You learn what a horse eats. And you learn then how to ride properly. It is the same way with higher consciousness. There are many different 'muscles' in the body of higher consciousness, and we learn to exercise all of them. If you learn to exercise only the left arm, the right arm becomes weak; it is important to exercise both arms. You understand the physical plane. You are now learning how to dance with the higher energies. You are learning about the subtler bodies. You are learning about the luminous fibers of your being, the web of power. And the web of power can be used in many ways. You can use it to hold you as you cross a great abyss. Someday, you will be able to walk across even Langford's crevice."

I stared at her, my eyes wide. "What do you mean, walk across Langford's crevice? It is hundreds of feet deep!"

"Yes, you can learn to throw your web of power, your luminous fibers, across great distances. You can move the fibers up to the top of a tree, and walk on those fibers from the bottom to the topmost branches of the tree without falling, without hurting yourself. That will come later. Now you are learning spirit flight. Whether you know it or not, your spirit shield grabs onto some of your luminous fibers as it moves out into the universe. That luminous fiber is never let go of—it is attached to the physical body like a silver thread. You follow it back. It is like a scent, like the way a dog finds its way home by instinct. In fact, it will feel to you like instinct, but really it is the luminous fibers that bring you home. Next time—tonight or in a few days—you move out of your body into spirit flight, you will see what I mean. You can go very, very far away, yet you can come back simply by using your intent."

"But that still does not tell me, Grandmother, what I can do with this."

"What you can do now is enjoy it, enjoy a new dimension in your life. The real use of spirit flight is to help you understand that we do not die. I've spoken of this before. If you learn and if you are lucky, the spirit shield goes on from one lifetime to another."

"But the Church says that we only have one life, that when we die, we go to heaven or hell depending on whether we have been good people or not," I said.

"Yes, that is one way to look at reality, but after last night I do not know how you could believe that. You now see that your spirit goes on. Your physical body could die while you were up at the ceiling. You would not have felt it. It would not have affected you; you would have gone on. Your luminous fibers would have changed position. They would have moved toward the Old One, and you would have been drawn toward the light."

"You mean when you die, you just move on toward God? But is that not just like going to heaven?"

"Yes, in a sense it is, and in a sense that is just another way of explaining that leaving the physical form is heaven, is it not? You have escaped the pain, the confinement, of this life. We are in a war against ignorance, and many people die of ignorance. That is something you must understand—that if we have a chance to work together for a lifetime, you will never die of ignorance."

I took this all in, watching the old woman as she ate her cake and got up now and then to stoke the fire. I let her words just sink into me, and I realized fully that she was right, that we were part of something great. I realized that I knew very little of what creation was really all about.

"Grandmother, why are we here?" I finally asked her. "Why are we in England? Why was I born? Why were you born? And why do so few people know about the things that you know about?"

Grandmother chuckled to herself. "People do not know of the things that I am teaching you because they are afraid. You overcame your fear, because something in your heart knows that truth is what is important in this life. Many people feel that following rules is the only thing that is important. Women and men of power want to understand the magic of the universe. They want to understand and live within the light of God, within the light of creativity. They want to understand the extraordinary mysteries that encompass our lives, so that they can be more perfect human beings. Truly, Catherine, we are, each and every one of us, a reflection of God, and that is all we are. We are mirrors of that great brilliance.

"To limit yourself to one set of beliefs, to limit your wisdom to what is known in one time and place, is pure ignorance. There are many times and many places. That is something I want you to explore in your spirit flight. I want you to move around all of Europe, and you will begin to see that people live differently. They all think they are living right—and maybe they are, for them—but none of these ways is the way of ultimate truth. They are all just living. Gaining knowledge of all the ways that people live is a great tool to help you begin to understand that we are here for only a moment, and in the blink of an eye our life will be over. You have a chance in this lifetime, Catherine, to see what really is valuable and to take what is valuable and manifest it in your life. You have been born at a time when women are very restricted, and it is true that you must be very careful. But in your own being you can evolve. You can do it, Catherine. We can all do it, but it takes enormous courage."

Grandmother reached over and placed her old, wrinkled hand on mine. "Tonight," she said, "when you are getting ready for sleep, when you are getting ready for your dreaming, imagine your luminous fibers. Loosen them, and allow your spirit shield to shine through them. Make the spaces between your fibers so large that you could stick your hand right through them. Try that tonight. Let yourself go. Let your spirit go beyond your home, beyond your village, beyond even the boundaries of England. Move out into space, and find another world. Explore it a bit. Remember, when you feel the tugging on the muscles just above your navel, you should return. All you need do is intend to go back into your body. Remember who you are, and do not be frightened, for you are going to learn many things in the next few weeks.

"Your real training has begun, Catherine. Stay strong, and remember to be thoughtful of your family. Do not frighten them by being different to them. They are only doing what they know how to do. They do not understand your world, but they give you great security and great power in the physical world. They are fine people, and they do good things for many. It is important that you do not upset them. Any knowledge of what we are doing would frighten them. You need not burden them with this knowledge, because they truly would not know what to do with it. Part of your power—and part of the cross that you have to bear—is the loneliness of the path. It is a dark time for England. You must remember that. Just be your usual self, do what your mother asks, and do not argue with her. Let them be who they are. It is all they know. Remember, they do not have to be like you; somehow because of the brilliance of your light and beauty, they will be affected by you. The effect will be subtle, but somehow some of your wisdom will transfer to them. Do not be impatient. I know having to keep secrets worries you, and you think you are deceiving your family. And I guess in a way you certainly are, but it is not something that you do to hurt them—or anyone.

"We must understand that we are living in difficult times. Remember that a woman of power needs to take power. It is never given to her. We are living in a world ruled by men. Power is not given to women. Woman once did have great power. In the old days of Wyrrd, woman had power. The family lines would often follow the woman; the woman chose her husband. But that is all gone now. People would destroy anyone who spoke to the spirits living in the trees and in the animals and in the stones. You must remember in your heart that a tree is no less alive than you are. But people do not understand that. They have forgotten the source of power. They have forgotten that power comes from woman, from this great Mother Earth. You understand in your heart, and you protect her, but to protect her is to protect yourself.

"You are not out in the world to hold up the sword as do the men you know. You are here to nourish knowledge and to keep it hidden for now. There will come a time—and you will be involved in that time—when this knowledge will go out into the world, when you will be able to speak to many people. There will be a time in a land far away from here when you will have a chance to teach what you are going to learn in this lifetime. So do not be sad. Hold tight inside to the understanding that you are part of the old ones. God is within you to make you strong, to help you through this transition.

"In your spirit flight you are closer to God than you have ever been. Handle it with care. Tell no one, because to do so would bleed the energy from your endeavor. Hold your power, my daughter. Now your work really begins. Stand in the position of a woman of Wyrrd, a young woman, an apprentice, but nevertheless a woman of Wyrrd. You are beginning to follow an ancient tradition. You are moving down the lineage. This is your destiny. Tread your path carefully and with love."

We sat for several minutes without saying a word. Then I leaned forward intently and asked, "Grandmother, when I go into my spirit flight am I moving into the past or the future?" The old woman laughed a little as she looked at me. "Why are you laughing?" I asked.

"Human beings always try to make things more difficult than they really are. No, you are not moving into the future or the past, although you could do that."

"You mean, I will just stay in the present time if I leave England in spirit flight?"

"Oh, yes, you will be in present time, but — "

"But what?" I asked.

"But you can move into the future or past."

"How can I do that, Grandmother?"

"It is difficult to explain, my daughter, but when you are in the world of spirit flight, you are out of time."

"What do you mean, 'out of time'? How could that be?" I was suddenly very confused.

"Time has to do with this physical reality." Grandmother knocked on the table with her knuckles then ran her fingers up and down her arm. "This is all relative. This is all part of you and me sitting here thinking that we are separated."

"But we are separated, Grandmother. You are sitting over there, and I am sitting here."

"Has it ever occurred to you that that is not how things are?" the old woman asked.

"No, Grandmother."

"Well, you might think about it, my daughter. In a way we have always 'been' and we will always 'be' and everything that has ever happened is happening right now. You could think of it in terms of layers of one reality here, just like this honey cake. This is the layer" — she pointed to the cake — "on the bottom." And then she pointed to the honey filling. "Now this filling could be the astral level where you are moving into spirit flight. I don't mean that the astral plane is over here," she said, pointing to the whole area of the room then tapping the table, "and that this is the physical reality over here. One layer is on top of another. There is density, a thickness, to life, and we ordinarily experience only this bottom piece. And we call that life, when actually there is a whole cake here. You can taste just the bottom and say, 'Oh, what a good cake.' Or you can taste the honey filling and the cake on top of that and get the whole sense of cakeness."

We laughed together at her story.

"But it really is true, Catherine. You must understand that there is more to life than what you see. From where you are standing, anything is possible."

I said nothing, but I watched, fascinated, as her eyes reflected the light of the lowering sun slanting through the windows. For a moment she looked like a hawk, her eyes turning yellow, flashing with red sparks just for a moment. I blinked, and the vision was gone. As I kept staring at her, Grandmother started to giggle.

"Yes, my daughter, we all have many forms."

She stood up. "That is enough talk for today, Catherine. It is time that you find your way home, so your parents will not be worried about you and will not notice how long you have been here." She put my cape over my shoulders.

I went outside, got on my horse and rode at a brisk trot down the road toward home. Pinewood smoke scented the damp air. For the first time in my life I could not wait to get home, eat, and go to bed.

CHAPTER 14

THE
PRESENCE
OF
LIFETIMES

Who follows the pattern
and waits not at any edge but in the reclamation
of distances
is born of need
and thanks the holy priestesses
questioning every solitude
holding knowledge pouring
the sand through glaze fingers
and tries
like the tune of an old song
that lives only in currents of air
in boxed memory
in ground fires
to sing the desperate anthem
anew.

ONE MORNING A FEW days later I awoke to find my mother sitting at the end of my bed looking down at me, a curious expression on her beautiful face. Her golden brown hair, plaited, was held with a silver clip.

"You have changed much lately, Catherine." I held my quilt up to my chin.

"I have?" My voice sounded more like a squeak. I blinked, trying to wake up. I was always nervous around my mother. She was very cool and remote. I never knew, really, what she was thinking.

"How have I been different?" I finally asked.

My mother looked at me for a long time saying nothing. Finally she shook her head.

"I guess the difference is that you seem happier. Your father and I would like you to know that we are pleased."

I heaved a sigh of relief. "Yes, Mother, I am happier. My horse makes me very happy. Thank you for giving him to me."

"Yes, you spend a great deal of time riding your horse. I hope you are careful. It is not that we do not love you, Catherine, it is just that people in our position have many obligations. Your father and I have many things to attend to. I know you understand."

Actually, I had always felt very hurt and lonely when my parents' obligations left me to my own devices. Now for the first time in my life I truly was relieved to be left alone. I gave my mother a big smile and kissed her on the forehead.

"Mother, I will be just fine. I am much happier now that I can go out and ride my horse and enjoy the countryside."

"Yes, you have always enjoyed nature. I am glad that you are finding such happiness in it. Enjoy it, because one day you may have to go to London to be received at Court."

"Oh, Mother, no! I could never be away from my beloved countryside. I could never be away from you and my horse. It would break my heart. Please, do not ever send me away." I had a horrible feeling of desolation at the very thought of being torn away from Grandmother. Tears welled up in my eyes. I could see the surprise on my mother's face.

"Why, Catherine, I thought you would be so happy to go away to London. Life at Court is the dream of all young girls like you."

"Well, it is not my dream, Mother. Please, just let me stay here. I will do whatever you want me to do."

My mother lowered her long, beautiful eyelashes, then looked up at me quizzically, as if I were a strange creature that she could never understand. I just hoped that she would forget the whole idea of London. After a time, she patted the top of my head, gathered her skirts, and walked out of the room, saying over her shoulder as she left, "Catherine, you certainly are a strange one." She closed the door behind her.

I looked around at my beautiful room—the silk tapestries on the walls, the frescoes on the ceiling, the paintings of my ancestors that hung on either side of the window that looked out on the grounds, the gently swaying trees that led down to a pond. I knew I was lucky to live in such a house and to have a chance to be at Court, but I wanted none of it. All I wanted was to be with Grandmother to learn the way of Wyrrd, to become a woman of power. I had no interest in being presented to the King and the Queen. I had no interest in the excitement of life at Court. But I knew my family's obligations: one day I might be torn away from Grandmother and have to live in London. I might have to take my place at Court one day. The thought of it terrified me. I could not imagine living without the old woman somewhere very near me.

I quickly dressed in my riding clothes and took up my cape. I had a couple of hours free. I ran downstairs and out to the stables. I went in and petted my horse's nose as James placed the saddle firmly on his back. He nickered softly. I brushed his face and his neck, and he pulled on my pocket with his teeth.

"If anyone asks after me, James, I will be back in an hour or so."

I jumped on my horse, and we raced off down the road. It was a beautiful morning. The robins and sparrows were chirping, and white, puffy clouds dotted the azure sky.

. . .

"Why is it that women have no say in the world, that they cannot choose what they want to do?" I asked indignantly as I sat down with Grandmother at the wooden table.

"My child, what has happened? You look flushed, upset."

"This morning my mother told me that I may have to go to London soon. I may have to be received in Court."

"My child, you must live your life. Whatever is going to happen is right for you. You must not try to change the course of time. The Fates will dictate what your life is to be. You will have learned much with me by the time you leave. You will have learned spirit flight. You can come to work with me in spirit time."

"You mean I could come to see you in my dreams, come to you in my spirit body?" I smiled. "That is possible, is it not, Grandmother? But we could not sit like this. We could not smell the beautiful flowers. We could not work in the forest at night. I could not see Anne."

"You could do all those things, Catherine, but it would be different. Yes, it would not be exactly the same, but at least I could teach you some things."

"Grandmother, you have such powers. Is there not some way that you could keep me here? I do not want to go to London. It frightens me. I know that I will die there."

"What you just said brings up something you need to know, my child. Whenever you are traveling in your spirit flight and you see someone who, perhaps, is in pain or needs you in some way, before you move into the energy field of that person on this plane or on any other plane, remember that you must always ask the guardians if you may pass."

"What guardians, Grandmother? You mean there are actual guards at the door like knights?"

Grandmother laughed. "Well, they are not exactly knights, but they may be. They could take any form. They may be wolves. They may be in the form of bears. They could be just people, but you will know that they are the guardians of that person, of that being. And you must be sure that you honor them and ask them if you may pass. If they say no, then there is nothing you can do even if you want to heal someone of a terrible disease. If the guardians say that you cannot pass, whatever is happening to that person is karmic, part of a past debt in life that must be paid by that person and that person alone. And you must not tamper with whatever it is. It is law, and it has always been that way, Catherine."

"I understand, Grandmother. I will be careful. Thank you."

Grandmother gazed at me for some time. "Remember," she finally said, "that your spirit knows no limits. There are no boundaries to your being. You are part of infinity. In the physical aspect of your life, you are limited. You have commitments. There are rules that restrict you. You are a woman in a man's world, and you must do certain things, but you have chosen to be born into the world at this time for a reason. There must be things that you need to learn about the world that exists today. Perhaps you are trying to learn to fly. Perhaps you are trying to learn to be free in your spirit. The more constricted your life is on a physical plane, the more you are going to want to break free of those boundaries and give wings to your being in spirit flight.

"When you go to sleep tonight and for the next few nights, practice all that you have been learning, and practice moving out of England altogether. See what it feels like. Experience deep in your soul the different dimensions of reality, so that one day you will be able to teach what you have learned — maybe in this lifetime, maybe not, but one day you will be able to teach what you have learned, and you will change the course of many people's lives."

I studied her face, not really knowing what to say. Finally I found my voice. "Grandmother, I cannot really imagine ever being a teacher or bringing inspiration into people's lives, but at the same time, when you say those things, deep inside I am moved to tears. Somehow I know that there is truth to what you say. I do not know how I know it, but I do."

"You know because your destiny has begun to unfold, and because we have been together before."

"But how can that be, Grandmother? We are not of the same family."

"No, perhaps not in this lifetime, but in other lifetimes we will meet again, and we have worked together before now." She winked at me. "Perhaps you were my teacher in another lifetime."

"Oh, Grandmother, it would be wonderful to believe that I would see you in other lifetimes, but it is so hard for me to believe. I hear your words, but I find it hard to accept their truth — that we have been together before." I hesitated for a moment. "I must say it is odd, though, that what you teach me seems like second nature, like something I have truly done before."

"Catherine, it is important for you to see that truth is always the same. Truth is what is. No matter what name you give it, what religion you call it, the truth is that the great beings, the conscious beings that have been on this planet are reflections of the Old One, reflections of God. The religions that are built around them often do not accurately pass on what the great teachers taught. It is important for you to see that truth is the same throughout the ages. It makes no difference what time or place you live in. What matters is that you become enlightened, and that is truly all that matters."

Grandmother took my hand and led me outside to the large alder that grew in the corner of her garden. As reverently as if she were offering a piece of her own body to the tree, she placed a sparrow feather into a hole in the bark.

"Have you ever heard of the tree of life, Catherine?"

"Is that not an ancient sacred symbol, a religious symbol?"

"Yes, my child, the tree of life teaches about the evolution of the spirit. Many years ago my teacher gave me a deck of cards. She called it simply the Power Deck. It is filled with knowledge for a specific purpose, for learning."

"You mean these cards are not intended to be a game?"

"No, not exactly. Just as the idea of the tree of life is a way of seeing a system of power and sacred flow, so are these cards a way of finding the source of truth within oneself. My teacher taught me many things about the tree of life through my understanding of what was written on the cards. Would you care to see them?"

"Yes." I was very excited and sat down on the grass with Grandmother. She reached into a deep pocket and produced a lovely carved box. She laid the box in front of me and nodded. A pleasant breeze had come up from the south filling my senses with lavender perfume. I placed my fingers gently on the box cover and traced what appeared to be ancient and worn runelike designs. A beautiful tree carved with exquisite detail was at the center of the cover. I picked up the box and opened it slowly as if I expected something to jump out at me. Inside, it was lined with red velvet. The cards were made from a material that could have been thinly pressed wood or leather. Inlaid on one side of the cards were beautiful pictures.

"Pick the cards, and think of a question you would like answered," Grandmother said. "Handle them carefully, they are very old. Treat them with the highest respect, for they are very sacred. As you think of a question, know that the cards are reading your spirit."

As I mixed the cards I noticed that the picture on each card was different. Each picture was of mountains, clouds, or animals, and each one held a message.

"Keep the picture side up as you work," Grandmother instructed.

I decided on a question and told her.

"Now, fan the cards out on the grass in front of you. Holding your palm slightly above them, pick the card that calls you and read the answer to your question. But first, remember that in this teaching the cards represent your outer body and the message represents the truth of spirit. It is the same with the tree of life. The cards teach that ultimately your spirit and your body are one," Grandmother touched the alder with her fingers, "just as the body and the spirit of this tree are one."

I held my outstretched hand over the cards. I felt uncanny heat from them, but one card with beautiful gilt flowers on it caught my attention. I picked it out of the others and turned it over. The message was penned in large, gold brushstrokes: "In death is the secret to life."

The message so directly answered my question that my mouth fell open. Grandmother giggled to herself a little at my astonishment.

"Do you wish to share your question with me?"

"Yes. I asked, What is the secret to a happy life?"

"See, the Power Deck never lies."

"How do the cards teach us about the tree of life?"

"Like the tree of life, the cards teach us about mediations between the life forces of the land and all forms of life. They teach us that we are all one. In that oneness we protect the powers of the land. There are magical keys in the Power Deck. These keys unlock the gateways to the mysteries of truth. Each time we study and use the Power Deck, we create light like the sparks from a fire. These sparks revitalize the life force that has been given away to us by the land so that we may live."

"Tell me more about how study relates to the earth, Grandmother."

"If you ask about sacred study, and I assume you do, I must tell you that the source of all power is hidden in our mother, the land. To live we must partake of our mother's body. To engage in sacred study completes the circle. Studying or using the cards of wisdom, learning more of truth, gives off light. The beings of the earth live in a give and take, a flow of light, that becomes life force and then becomes love. It is law."

I gently collected the cards and placed them back in their box, reluctant to hide their beauty. Grandmother put them back in her pocket.

"Will I be allowed to use them again?"

"Yes, Catherine, but at the moment we have much to do. I wanted you to meet the wise cards because one day you will have your own. Simply think about them. That is enough for now. Come, the sun is getting higher. It is time for you to go. For there to be enlightenment," she went on, "there has to be a modicum of comfort, and if you do not get home right now, you are not going to be comfortable, because your family is going to worry about you. There may be trouble, so get on your horse and gallop on home."

"Yes, Grandmother, you are right."

I gave her a big hug and a kiss on the cheek. Mounting my horse, which had been grazing happily in front of her cottage, I rode home through the clear morning air.

CHAPTER · 15

THE
ABYSS

Nothing works like
the thin line of distinction.
The essence of grace
is moving without sound
and speaking in a dark wind.
So why do we consider ourselves enemies?
And why is my inner life
drowning?

THE NEXT THING I knew, I was awake, lying on my back on sheepskins in the Dreamlodge in Manitoba. Rain pelted down on the exterior covering of the lodge making a staccato sound. Every once in a while a drop of water would land in the fire, and the fire would hiss and spit. I looked up through the smoke hole at the dark sky. Rain clouds moved swiftly across the moon. I lay back with my head on the blankets, trying to clear my thoughts. My head ached, and my eyes were hot.

Moments later Agnes parted the blankets that covered the doorway. She came in very quietly watching my face and examining the energy field around my body.

Seating herself next to me, she reached over to stroke my forehead. "We could not wake you. We have been very concerned."

Her hands and fingers felt very warm, because my body was very, very cold. She began to rub my hands between her palms, which felt like worn leather.

"Are you all right, Lynn?"

"I think so, Agnes, except that I feel woozy."

Agnes laughed at my choice of words and poked me in the ribs. "I think you're going to be just fine," she said.

"How long have I been gone, Agnes?" I asked.

"Too long. I want to make sure that you never do this again." She tapped my chest with her finger, then removed the necklace. "We must make sure that you know when to return. The luminous fibers will pull you back when it is time."

"Oh, Agnes, I am so glad to be home! It is very beautiful there. Grandmother is wonderful, but it's so strange, so different from anything I've ever experienced. It's alien—cold, in a way. But I'm learning much; I'm learning things that I don't even know in this lifetime."

"Well, that's good," Agnes said. "It's about time you learned a few things." She laughed at me, and pulled me to my feet. I could barely stand.

"You never answered me, Agnes. How long have I been gone?"

"You've been gone for a couple of days, my daughter. Never again will you do this. You scared us all, even Ruby."

Agnes and I went to my altar and said prayers to the spirits for helping me on my journey. We smudged the Dreamlodge with pungent cedar smoke and smudged ourselves. Then Agnes made a paste of *pajo*, or corn pollen, water, and another herb that I did not recognize; she stripped off my clothes and rubbed it all over my body. At first it felt granulated and rough, but after a few moments it began to feel soothing and warm. As

Agnes rubbed it in, her eyes were closed, and she was singing under her breath in her native tongue. I knew better than to ask her what she was doing until later.

She paid special attention to my heart area and my navel and pressed the paste into those areas. I began to realize that I felt bruised there, almost as if I had been punched in my solar plexus.

"This will help heal you," Agnes said, keeping her eyes closed.

The wind was blustering outside, rattling the Dreamlodge structure against its poles. My teeth began to chatter in tune with the fluttering of the wind. My legs felt like tiny reeds in the wind as I began to quiver. Agnes placed her hands under my arms to help me up and led me out of the Dreamlodge and up toward the cabin.

We stopped at a quiet place on the creek where it widened and formed a pool with a mossy bottom. With one swift motion Agnes dunked me in the creek water head first. My entire body was submerged. I felt her hand on my back but did not have the strength to fight her off. She grabbed my neck and the hair on the back of my head and pulled my head up, looked into my eyes, and dunked my head under again. I spluttered under water. As she lifted my head again I coughed and sputtered, furious but at last fully awake.

She began wiping all the *pajo* off me and left me standing there naked in the creek while she went over and cut three or four willow branches. As I came out of the creek, she began to dust me with the leaves and the branches, slapping me until I stung from head to toe.

"There," she said, "like new." She stepped back and admired her work.

My entire body was pink. I took a deep breath and glared at her. "I suppose I should say thanks," I said.

Agnes giggled. "You're at least back in one piece now."

She grabbed my clothes, which she had dropped on the ground, and handed them to me. Quickly I put them back on, feeling warm and comforted by the soft cotton.

· · ·

As we entered the cabin, Ruby was sitting at the table, and July was outside chopping wood. Ruby sensed me in the way that she does — as if she "sees" you to your bones — and started to laugh.

"Well, you sure do look weird," she said, slapping her thighs and pounding her fist on the table.

"Very cute, Ruby. Thanks a lot."

I sat down at the table, still feeling weak in the knees. Agnes placed bread and smoked fish on a plate in front of me.

"Eat," she said.

I suddenly realized that I had never been so hungry in my entire life. I inhaled the food almost as quickly as she put it in front of me.

"Eat much?" Ruby growled as she looked at me stuffing my face.

"You'd be hungry too, Ruby, if you hadn't eaten in two days."

"Well, I also wouldn't be so stupid as to stay in the Dreamtime for two days. You did frighten us."

"Ruby, I didn't mean to be gone that long. I don't know why I didn't come back. I guess there was just a lot happening."

"Well, it was sure peaceful around here, I can say that," Ruby said with a shrug.

Then Ruby became very serious, her eyes reflecting the sunlight like the silvery surface of the creek that I had just been dunked in. She got up from her chair and walked around me holding her hands about five inches away from my body. She ran her hands up and down very slowly looking up at the ceiling of the cabin with that faraway gaze that was so eerie, that interior vision that I could never share with her. It always made me a little uneasy. She looked so formidable, somewhere between a human being and a wild animal. Her hair fringed out around her face, braided down her back. She wore a heavy necklace of turquoise that contrasted vividly with her red shirt. Her face was tanned to a dark brown, creased and lined like the bed of a dry lake. It was awe-inspiring to feel the power emanating from this woman. When she moved into her shaman place, she radiated heat like a stove. I sat still wondering what she was looking for.

"There is a map in your energy field," Ruby said as if she were answering the question in my mind. "It is the map of your awareness. It tells me of your journey."

After several minutes I couldn't stand it anymore. "Ruby, what are you seeing?"

"It's interesting that you use the word *seeing* with me, an old blind woman, because in fact that is exactly what I'm doing. I am looking at your luminous fibers to see if any are injured. I am watching the reflections of your life force, and they are fine. They are very good—still weak, but becoming stronger.

"Now you must learn a new lesson. There is such a thing as awareness. We talk of it often. We use the word easily. But we do not understand the importance of awareness on a level other than physical reality. To become aware of your luminous fibers and their strength and power in other dimensions is to become aware on many levels. You are strengthening your awareness in the other circles of power besides this one."

Ruby made an expansive gesture in the air, a large circle with her arms. "There is another hoop of reality. That is where you have been. In that

reality you are developing an awareness, but you must not lose the awareness of your physical reality, or you will lose your life," Ruby said, tapping me on the shoulder.

"But how do I maintain awareness on two levels at the same time?"

Ruby sat down slowly across from me looking off to the left as if she
were staring out the window.

"Can you explain to me what it is like to be dreaming in your Dreamlodge and experiencing something in long-ago England? Can you tell me
how you do this?" Ruby asked, raising her eyebrows.

I thought for a long time and realized that I didn't have much to say.
"Ruby, I can describe the experience. I can talk about the experience, but
I certainly can't explain how I got there."

"And therein lies the problem of spiritual teaching," Ruby said, shaking her head. "I can describe to you how you looked lying there in the
Dreamlodge, but I cannot explain how you left your body in your spirit
shield and moved to another time frame. This is something that is part of
the unknowable. Agnes and I can take you there. We can give you the
'muscles,' the ability to exercise your luminous fibers. We can take you
there, but only you can make it happen—you and the Great Spirit. In the
same way, there is no explaining creation. Perhaps you understand it only
when you join the Great Spirit for the last time."

I thought for a long time about what she had said. I stared at her, taking another big bite of bread and washing it down with the tea Agnes had
placed in front of us.

"Then it is a wordless wisdom, Ruby, because I have a feeling inside
me that tells me how to move into that time frame. But I can't explain it
to you. I can say that there is a tension around my solar plexus. I could tell
you that my head aches and then becomes light, that I hear a cracking
sound somewhere in my back. I can tell you that it's my shaman's intent
that gets me there, but I don't know *how* it gets me there. That frustrates
me greatly, because I want to be able to explain it."

I took another bite. Agnes laughed at my voracious appetite and
pinched my cheek.

"My daughter, this is the frustration of all people of power. We know
each other by the magnificent light, by the luminous egg that surrounds
us. We can see each other and identify each other, but we cannot begin to
explain how this happens. We cannot even explain how the spirit shield
moves beyond your luminous fibers. We can describe the experience and
what it looks like, and that is all. After you have finished your lunch and
rested, we are going to take you outside and show you something more
about your fibers of power. We are going to show you how to tug on
them, how to feel them with your hands, because if you cannot feel them

with your hands, it is possible that you will not be able to do as we have advised and come back sooner next time. It is very dangerous for you to have stayed away for two days. Something could really have happened to you."

Her words struck me with terror. My face must have gone ashen, because both Agnes and Ruby began to laugh.

"Don't worry, my daughter, we would have found a way to get you back, but it is important that you do this on your own."

After eating I lay down on the bed for what I thought would be only a few minutes. I awoke hours later to Agnes shaking my shoulders. Through the window I saw the orange glow of the sun as it went down over the horizon. I sat up in alarm.

"Agnes, I didn't mean to go to sleep all those hours!"

"Come. It is time," she said very seriously.

She threw my parka to me, and I got up, trying to shake the sleep out of my eyes and my consciousness. She handed me a piece of deer jerky, and we walked quickly out of the cabin, shutting the door behind us.

The trees and the grass were tinged with a pink orange light from the streaks of color in the sky above. The wind had died down, and it was very still.

"It is a good night." Agnes looked at me.

"Where is Ruby?" I asked.

"She is in the canyon."

I lifted my eyebrows. We had not worked there for a long time. The canyon in the rocks behind the cabin was some distance away, and we never went into it unless we were going to work. It was an initiation canyon, a very sacred place that had been used by Agnes and her teachers for centuries.

Agnes was walking at a stiff clip. I followed, scrambling up and down boulders, slipping and sliding on shale until, finally, we reached the canyon. The golden orange ball of sun settled down over the horizon leaving a purple sky behind. The top of the canyon was still rimmed in gold. Ruby was standing on the opposite side of an abyss, holding her arms up to the setting sun. There was such silence in the wilderness that I could hear the slight movements of her feet in the shale. I could hear her singing to the setting sun. Her voice echoed around and around in the canyon. This was the canyon where I had done the mother rattle ceremony many long years ago, where the water babies had presented themselves to me, the water spirits that have been my allies all this time. I had no tobacco or cornmeal with me, so I pulled a piece of my hair and offered it to the canyon, to this sacred place of spirit.

Agnes tugged on my sleeve. "Come," she said.

Instead of walking down the trail into the canyon, which we had always done, she led me around on a precipitous trail just below the rim. I do not like heights, and I did not want to look down. I placed one foot in front of the other and followed her carefully. As we rounded a boulder I found a ledge with a small cave behind it like a cupped hand settled into the rock, turning dark with shadow as the purple sky began to slowly fade. I was grateful for the long twilight in the far north. I knew we would have some time to do our ceremony, whatever it was, and still have light. The entire area was bathed in a purple iridescent glow.

As we came to the ledge in front of the cave, Agnes bent down and with her fingers brushed away tiny pebbles, pieces of mica, that were resting in two shallow indentations in the surface of the stone. It looked like a platform, as if you would put a statue there. Then I realized with surprise that the indentations were two footprints in the stone.

Agnes grabbed my arm. "Come," she said. "It is the perfect time."

She had me place my feet in the footprints. They felt comfortable there, and I realized there must have been many feet there before mine. I was reminded of Australia and the Woman's Rock, where there had been two indentations for hands that fit as if they had been made for me. These indentations had been used for ceremony for thousands of years. A thrill rushed through me, and I began to feel the energy of Mother Earth coming through my feet and moving up my spine to circulate through my body.

"Loosen your knees. Do not stand with your knees locked; you cut off the energy," Agnes said, rapping the back of my knees with the short stick she was carrying. "Be aware, my daughter, of the wind. Look at grandmother hawk circling above you."

I looked up to see the golden-edged wings of a giant red-tailed hawk that was circling effortlessly in the drafts above me. She screamed her hunting cry and looked down toward the earth hundreds of feet below. I looked across the abyss at Ruby, who was also standing with legs gently apart on a similar ledge with a cave behind her that was lost in shadow. The abalone-shell disk that hung from the turquoise necklace around her neck shone brilliantly in the sunset light.

"Concentrate on Ruby," Agnes said. "Look into her eyes. Do not blink. Cross your eyes as you have been taught. Cross your eyes and continue to look into Ruby's face as best you can. Open yourself. Move completely into your shaman stance. Let all thoughts fall away. Let your conscious mind be clear. Do not let the words in your mind pull your attention away."

After a long time had passed Agnes began to massage the back of my neck. After some more time she punched the upper part of my back with her fist. On the physical plane I hardly felt the crack of her knuckles, but on some other level I felt as if my spirit shield had been pushed out beyond my body suddenly and with extraordinary impact. I heard a loud cracking sound that seemed to run down my back. My whole body began to shiver.

"Pay attention," Agnes ordered. "Do not take your eyes off Ruby. Pay attention. Do not indulge yourself in fear."

I was teetering on the edge of the precipice. For a moment I was afraid I would just fall forward and plunge to the bottom of the canyon and certain death. And then something began to happen. I began to feel a tugging on my solar plexus. For a moment I thought I could see shining threads attached to the same spot on Ruby's body and reaching out across the abyss toward me. They quivered in the purple light, and for a moment, one moment, I thought they extended into my body at my navel. The moment I registered my surprise and excitement, the luminous fibers disappeared.

Agnes walloped me again on my back, and this time I felt as though I had lost consciousness. Somewhere I moved into that Dreamtime that I had been experiencing in England, but now I was not in England. I was somewhere out between where I stood and where Ruby stood in the abyss. I was as light as that hawk circling above me. Somehow I knew to grab hold of the luminous fibers that indeed were extending from one edge of the abyss to the other. It was not that I grabbed onto them with my hands or my fingers. I grabbed onto them with my intent, with the strength of will that lives in my solar plexus. I felt as if I were swinging like a tightrope walker who had lost her footing and was hanging by her fingers. My consciousness was gone. All that existed was pure space and energy and a deep red glow of light.

Again, Agnes walloped me, and this time I felt my consciousness awaken. I was standing again in my place, standing within the imprints in the stone. My body was shaking, but I stood my ground. I felt a hot pulsation around my navel area that hurt and began to itch. I wanted to tear at my flesh, but somehow I couldn't move my arms.

"Grab hold of the fibers," Agnes hissed in my ear. "Grab it right at your navel."

My spirit hands grabbed hold of the luminous cord magically attached to my navel. It shone purple in the light and felt like a silken cord. Suddenly it began to spin in my grip at an extraordinary rate as if the power of the entire universe were surging through it. The last thing I remember was looking up at the hawk circling above me screaming a welcome.

The next thing I knew I was back in my bed in Agnes's cabin. Agnes, Ruby, and July were sitting around me.

As I opened my eyes July said with great excitement, "Lynn, can you teach me how to do that? You walked halfway across the abyss."

"What abyss?" I asked, sounding to myself as if I were drunk.

"The canyon," Ruby said.

With the sound of her voice my head swiveled to look at her, and I remembered everything. Dimly in my mind I remembered walking off the edge of the abyss toward Ruby, and then I remembered nothing else except the sound of the hawk screeching high above me, as if welcoming me into spirit flight. I closed my eyes and did not wake until the following morning.

Agnes sat next to me on the bed offering me a cup of tea.

"Agnes, I need a day off," I said.

My body felt as battered as if I had fallen to the bottom of the abyss. I ached in every muscle and bone.

Agnes laughed. "Come. We'll go on a picnic down by the pond today. We will relax. We will find some wild chamomile for your eyes," she said, and placed her warm fingers on my forehead.

C H A P T E R · 1 6

SPIRIT CIRCLE

And who are you
far into the heat?
I will not answer
way over in the milkweed field
because the fever is here
where spring begins.
So what good will truth do
not a thin voice to guide the eye
or how dark bones cover dark skin
and only then are we open to crying.
I am the one who says
prayer is touch.
You are the one who says
touch is prayer.
We sing of differences.
We are all together here.

Anne and I were staying with Grandmother in the stone cottage for two days until the new moon. Grandmother and I were preparing an early morning meal. It was unlike Anne not to be up before everyone, so I went into her room to see what was keeping her. I was alarmed to find her asleep. I went over and looked at her more closely fearing she might not be feeling well. She was moaning in her sleep and covered with perspiration. I placed the back of my hand on her brow. It was burning hot. I ran to tell Grandmother.

Moments later we had a pan full of cold water and were wringing out cloths to put on Anne's forehead. I was frightened. I looked at Grandmother for reassurance, but she did not notice me. She was preparing poultices of herbs to place over Anne's stomach and chest.

Several hours later Grandmother and I sat down at the kitchen table exhausted and worried.

"Grandmother, what is happening to her?" I asked.

"She is very ill. She has a very high fever; I suspect that she has sky sickness."

I was horrified, remembering a girl I had once known who had contracted this illness. The high fever had left the muscles on the right side of her body completely paralyzed. I knew that sky sickness could also kill you within days. "What can we do?" I asked.

"We will prepare a ceremony and a spirit circle," Grandmother said.

Her fingers moved over the grooves in the table. Her eyes held a faraway look, as if she were looking into another dimension for answers she could not find on this physical plane.

"You're a young apprentice, Catherine. I want you to watch what is going to happen to our friend Anne very closely. Anne has become ill because a spirit is attacking her. In some way she has welcomed that spirit. An attack like this does not happen without good reason."

My eyes widened, and my throat went dry. I didn't know what to say, so I said nothing.

"Do you notice how warm Anne has become, how her temperature has gone up?" Grandmother asked me. "There is a life force in all of us. The life force comes directly from the Goddess Mother, from God," Grandmother said. "It is a protection, a shield that protects the body from invasion. When an evil form of a spirit—a dwarf, a wyn, or an elf—attacks you with arrows of disease and negativity, the life force flames to protect your physical being from onslaught."

"So that is why her forehead is so hot?" I asked.

"Yes, Catherine, her spirit shield is burning like a flame, like a bonfire, to try and fend off this attack. It is an elf attack. If you wondered what I was doing a moment ago, I was traveling into the spirit world to find the track down which her soul was taken. It is being held by the elves. She has displeased them in some way. It is important that I find out how they have been displeased; then I will find her soul and return it to her. But it must be done quickly."

"How quickly?" I asked.

"Within the next two nights. The bonfire created within her by her own life force is not going to be able to burn with that intensity for long. It will burn itself out, and she will die. If that occurs, nothing can save her. Her spirit shield will work to help. Her intent is quite strong. She is trained enough."

"How does the spirit shield help, Grandmother? I don't understand fully. What is the difference between the spirit shield and life force?"

"The life force comes down from the Old One and infuses the physical body with life when a person is born onto this Mother Earth. It is after the person is born that the spirit shield is activated. The spirit shield that you have experienced shining through your luminous fibers is part of this lifetime and can move around in all dimensions if it is trained. When you die the spirit shield goes into the earth. When you die the life force goes back into the Old One. Occasionally, if someone is trained properly, the spirit shield can move on, as it is in this lifetime, to another lifetime. If you do your work well, Catherine, your spirit shield will follow you from lifetime to lifetime."

"That sounds very important," I said.

"It is important, my child, because if the spirit shield moves from one lifetime to another, it becomes educated. In answer to your question, the spirit shield helps by using its ability to remember and to use that knowledge—the knowledge stored within the shield. You have two minds. The inner mind is a soul mind. You make contact with that mind through your body, through your navel area. That is where magic enters you," the old woman said, poking my lower belly. "When you need knowledge that is in your spirit shield, you do not have to rely on your outer mind." Grandmother tapped her forehead.

"You mean, you might ask for an ability to work for you when you are sleeping and it would then proceed to help you?" I asked.

"Yes, and its intensity would depend on the intensity with which you worked on the task or the imprinting originally. It is very difficult to become enlightened in one lifetime. If the spirit shield continues to learn and you become conscious of this from one lifetime to another, the task of becoming enlightened is accelerated. We must try and preserve Anne's spirit shield from harm. It, too, can burn up in a spirit attack."

Suddenly I was very angry. I pounded my fist on the table. "Grandmother, how could an elf want to hurt her? *Why* would an elf want to hurt her? She is such a beautiful girl and such a good person."

"Somehow," Grandmother said, "and I don't know how yet, she has greatly offended the kingdom of elves. But we will restore her soul. Right now I want you to gather some herbs for me in the garden. I need to leave for a short time, Catherine. You take care of Anne. I am going to gather a few people. I am going to bring another woman of equal power. These are people I work with in the spirit circle, so do not be afraid. They would never betray our confidence together, and you must never tell anyone about them. When you meet them, when they leave, it should be as if you have never met them. I trust you, Catherine. I am trusting you with all our lives to keep our confidence. Do you understand?"

I looked solemnly into Grandmother's face. The intensity of her words was stronger than I had ever heard. I nodded my head yes and held my hand over my heart.

"You know you can trust me, Grandmother. Do not ever think about it again," I said with almost equal intensity—with all I could muster at the time.

That afternoon was spent between Anne's bed and the garden. I kept wiping the perspiration off her face and arms and placing cool poultices of lavender and other herbs over her eyes and chest. In between I would go out into the garden and carefully dig up herbs, keeping the roots intact, and bringing them into the house and preparing them as Grandmother had shown me. I was very careful. Some of them I was hanging up to dry. Some I was grinding. Some of the roots I was grinding together for poultices, others for ceremonial purposes. At one point the table was covered with blossoms of blue, yellow, red, and pink. It was festive and beautiful, and in a sense, I disliked destroying the blossoms. They were a magnificent testimony to life, and their power filled the room with a wonderful fragrance of spring. I prayed over them and thanked them for giving away so we could cure Anne of this terrible disease.

I was afraid for Anne. And I was afraid for myself, afraid to lose my friend—I had had so few. I knew that she was suffering greatly. I lit white candles in her room and prayed to all the spirits I knew, to the Mother Goddess to help her on her journey toward health.

Toward nightfall, I heard the clattering of hooves outside and thought that Grandmother had returned. But there was a knock at the door. I went over and opened it, and there stood the most handsome man I had ever laid eyes on. He was in his early twenties, tall and dark, and wearing leather breeches and tall boots. He was obviously of noble birth, and I thought that perhaps my family had sent him to spy on me.

I took a step back, about to close the door, but he smiled reassuringly. "You must be Catherine," he said.

"Yes," I stammered.

Behind him I saw Grandmother coming around the corner of the house and realized that this must be one of the people she had gone to collect.

"Are you — " I started to ask and stopped.

"Grandmother has asked me to join you in the spirit circle," he said with a twinkle in his eye.

I was completely disarmed and smiled back at him, quite relieved.

"For a moment I thought you — " I stopped myself again.

"I understand," he said, kissing the back of my hand as he raised it to his lips. "My name is Charles," he said. "Charles of Glastonbury at your service." He bowed his head.

My knees went weak as I gazed into his eyes and caught the scent of lemon on his skin. I must have stuttered as I backed away from the door to let him enter. Grandmother stood on the threshold with her hands on her hips and her head cocked to one side. She shook her head and said nothing, but her eyes said everything. I looked away from her steady gaze knowing that everyone in the room could see my cheeks blushing to fuchsia. I was so filled with the shyness and confusion of my own emotions that at first I did not even notice the woman who came in the door behind Grandmother. She was a noblewoman dressed in a beautiful, long velvet gown with a black veil. As she lifted her veil, I blinked in surprise; I had seen this woman many times at my parent's home.

"Lady Glastonbury." I bowed my head and curtsied.

"Catherine, how interesting to see you." She bowed to me as well. "Little Lady Catherine — it does not surprise me."

Thoughts fled through my mind — of evenings we had spent around the great table in the dining hall in my home, the many times that Lady Glastonbury and her friends had come to be with us. I had never dreamed that she was involved with the way of Wyrrd. I could not speak. Finally Lady Glastonbury reached out and touched me gently with her fingers.

"You may call me Alice," she said. "That will be sufficient. Come. Let us not forget the gravity of what we must do here. We must keep our wits about us. Forget about questions for now. We must save Anne's life, and to do this all of us must use our wills to the utmost." She put her arm around me and shook me gently.

I took a deep breath and walked with her into the kitchen. Grandmother turned around, still shaking her head, then came over to me and kissed me on my forehead. She looked at me strangely.

"Grandmother, what is it?" I asked her.

"Your history and your future have just revealed themselves to me. It is fine, my child. We will talk about it at another time. Alice is right. We must put aside any thoughts we have at this moment. Anne is very ill, and we must save her life. Tonight is the only chance we have; tomorrow will be too late."

The next hour or so was spent preparing the central chamber, taking out some of the furniture and putting it in the bedchambers, pushing the remaining furniture against the walls. It was a tiny room, but it would be large enough for what we needed, Grandmother said. Every once in a while I would catch Charles staring at me for a moment. My cheeks would flush crimson, and my heart would pound as I went on with my work.

By nightfall all the proper herbs had been hung from the rafters. Candles had been set out and lit. Bells and drums and the tools of the way of Wyrrd were set about on a table covered with fine linen cloth. I had gone down to the river, collected running water, placed it in brass bowls that shone in the firelight like the sun. Charles and Alice and Grandmother took out their swords and special ceremonial knives and placed them on the table with a looking glass next to the bowls of water. Grandmother told me to look at them—not to handle them, but to look at them carefully. Each one was carved with runes and symbols. Each had crosses and circles with various inscriptions on them, and I had no idea what they meant.

The room looked like the inside of a church with the candles glowing and flickering. Alice insisted that flowers should be set in the four directions of the room. It began to seem like a room set for a wedding, an evening wedding, a marriage of body and spirit. It was beautiful and eerie at the same time. Pungent herbs and incense smoke permeated the air. I was transfixed by the wonder of it all and both excited and frightened for my friend Anne. I wondered what was going to happen.

The four of us went into Anne's room, and wrapping her in her bedding and nightdress, we carried her very carefully to the center of the main room we had prepared for this ceremony. We laid her down on rugs and pillows on the floor, set candles around her, placed at her head bowls of running water that had been gathered from the stream. Then each of us in turn went to the altar, the table that had been laid with linen and candles and offerings, and said our prayers to the Old One, asking for power and for guidance from our allies on this journey. I was the last one to pray, and I fashioned my prayer after what had been said before me. This was all new to me and I understood very little, but I did sense the sacredness of the journey and I proceeded with that in mind.

Grandmother indicated a chair off to the right. I sat down there wondering if there was something I should do. Grandmother tended to Anne, as did Alice and Charles. They spent some time rubbing her with herbs and slapping the blankets that covered her with nettles and sweeping the ground around her with nettles as well. At one point Grandmother whispered to me that they were driving away any other spirits in the room that were of negative force.

Then Charles and Alice sat down at Anne's feet, and Grandmother slipped away. They began to chant in a Gaelic tongue. Their voices were rhythmic and the sound hypnotic. All of a sudden from outside I heard the strong flapping of wings. An extraordinary ruckus was going on outside the kitchen door. A large creature with the head of an owl, a white barn owl, and sleek feathers draped down its back and sides burst in through the door and leapt into the center of the room screaming like a hawk. As the creature swirled in front of us, surrounded by a halo of incense smoke, I picked out the figure of a woman, although her face was covered by the face of an owl, as if an actual owl's head had been made into a mask and its wings settled down over the side of her face and onto her shoulders. The woman held her arms up. On each arm was a falcon. They screamed into the still night air, piercing every corner of the room with their resounding cries. The birds flew into the air as the woman leapt and swirled and danced an extraordinary dance that was both frightening and fascinating at once. I had never seen anything like it. It seemed as if the woman herself were a bird swooping and dipping over Anne, as if Anne were her prey, and she was circling to light upon her. The falcons flew to the perches on either side of the altar as she whirled her arms and body in the air in a perfection of rhythm and movement.

Charles and Alice were sitting cross-legged, holding in their laps two drums made from a hollow oak branch. They beat on the drums in cadence, the beats accelerating and slowing to the dance of this extraordinary woman, truly a woman of Wyrrd. I became mesmerized by the movements, by the screams of the birds, and the rhythmic message from the drums like the heartbeat of Mother Earth. Every once in a while Gypsy cymbals would sound from under the feathers worn by the woman. She must have had them between her fingers. Every once in a while I would see a glint of light, as if from fire and sparks. It must have been the click of the cymbals. Her dance was Gypsy-like, but only in the sense that she was whirling as she danced, her skirts dusting the ground as she bent at the waist, swirling her arms over Anne's body as the falcons beat their wings almost in time to the beat of the drums.

I was also in awe of Charles and Alice. Alice I had seen in one sophisticated setting after another, a woman not unlike my own mother, always dressed in the most magnificent gowns, always drinking wine from the most magnificent crystal and silver. Here she was sitting on the floor of Grandmother's small stone house beating a drum in an ecstatic trance with the woman of Wyrrd. I was heady from it all.

I leaned back against the wall, realizing I was close to a trance-like state myself. Grandmother had told me to watch everything and remember, that she was going to ask me later about the ceremony. She had told me to stay in a state of deep meditation and to bring in as much power as I could, focusing my attention on my navel area and sending it out to Anne.

Finally, after what seemed like an hour of wild dancing and tumultuous sound, a cacophany of music and bird screams and yells from the woman, Charles and Alice laid down their drums and walked over to the woman, who had swooped down into a seated position at Anne's head, holding her arms out for the falcons to return to her wrists. She stroked each against her cheeks and then let them fly back to their pedestals. The birds became instantly subdued, as if they too were in a trance. They were very docile, though they were not hooded. They did not seem to be controlled, really, in any way at all. It was obvious that Alice and Charles had worked with them before, because when they raised their arms, the birds leapt right onto the patches of leather tied to their wrists. The birds gripped them firmly, behaving like tame sparrows as they were lifted and petted and then returned to their perches on the table. They lifted their wings once and spread them out, fluffing them, and then seemed to lower their heads in a posture of repose. Their eyes glittered like jewels in the candlelight. It was an impressive sight—two enormous falcons on either side of the beautiful table with white linen, candles, and silver and brass bowls sparkling in the firelight.

After a time the woman lifted her arms and began chanting in a language unfamiliar to me. I understood not a word. Then she crooned to the spirits in English as if she were seducing them in some way into being present. She motioned in the air, drawing designs to the sky. Every once in a while she would get up and whirl around beating the ground with nettle branches. Finally, she worked herself up to a fever pitch as she whirled and swirled around. Alice and Charles followed her movements, singing with her in this unfamiliar tongue. All three of them brushed Anne's body from time to time, sometimes using water and spraying it over her from head to toe, other times using something that looked like flour; occasionally they dipped a hand in a bowl of the ground herbs I had prepared earlier and dabbed them on her face and neck. All the while the bird woman continued with her swirling dance, her dance of light and power, the owl's head coming to life with every movement and its blind eyes glittering oddly in the reflected flames. The owl's cold beak thrust out over the forehead of the woman, throwing her face into deep shadow.

After half the night had passed, the owl woman threw back her cloak of feathers and took the owl head off her face. She swooned onto the ground and completely dissolved into a trancelike state. It was as if she had twisted down like a screw into a board and collapsed on the floor in a heap of feathers. I gasped. Why had it not occured to me? The owl woman was actually Grandmother. I had been so taken by the ceremony, so swept away by the emotion and the sounds and the unfamiliarity of what was happening around me that I had not even wondered why Grandmother had not returned. The old woman had moved powerfully through the ceremony, danced leaping into the air like a young man. I could hardly believe my eyes.

As Alice brushed by me, getting another bowl of water from the table, she whispered in my ear. "Do not take your eyes off Grandmother."

Alice stood before Grandmother and, dipping water from the bowl, she sprinkled it over Grandmother and Anne. "This is for the spirits of the north," she cried out. Taking more water she said, "And this is for the spirits of the east. And this is for the beings that live in the south." Taking more water she sprinkled it over the entire altar and the rest of the room. "This is for the spirits of the west who dwell in the land of death," she said and sat down again at Anne's feet. What happened next was an in- credible cacophony. All three were moaning and singing and chanting and moaning again to their own inner melody. They were all lost in trance. I found out later that they were journeying together to the land of the dead to retrieve Anne's soul, to make peace with the elves, to bring back her life.

At some point during this time all three made offerings to the elves, and they asked me to do the same. I offered herbs that had been given to me in a pouch, placing them on the altar along with food in silver platters and bowls, brass bowls of water, and clay dishes mounded with food and roots and herbs of all kinds. There was an unimaginable profusion of items they had brought together, things that had been kept in pouches I had never seen before, all kinds of magical symbols made out of brass, wood crosses, Goddess figures carved in wood, designs drawn on old parchments. And then finally, on the floor, where rugs had been rolled back, Alice and Charles drew several symbols in chalk. The white chalk glistened in the firelight as if it were luminescent. There was a star in a circle and then several symbols that I did not know in the four corners and in the center of the star. Next they laid herbs on the design, then took them off. They moved solemnly around it while Grandmother went into a trance again, moaning in a crouched position, the owl's head bobbing back and forth as her shoulders heaved. From time to time she would let out a cry that sounded like a hawk in flight.

I did not take my eyes off Grandmother, although her face was often obscured by shadow. I strained to see her. All of a sudden I began to see red sparks in the shadows. I strained to hear if she was clicking the finger cymbals again. Then I realized that Grandmother was beginning to stand up. Her body was moving in a circle along the ground like a screw being retracted from a board. Slowly her body began to swivel around and up. As her face moved in and out of shadow, I saw her turn from an ancient woman with a face of lines and wrinkles into a beautiful young woman.

I gasped and almost fainted myself, because the woman before me was the woman who had brought me to Grandmother, the woman I had seen on the jetty at the lake, the woman I had seen working with the falcons at the top of the hill. I was struck with terror. Grandmother had not prepared me for this. The area around my navel began to ache as the fibers of Wyrrd were yanked, and then I realized they were being tugged in the direction of Grandmother—but this wasn't Grandmother; this was someone else. No wonder Grandmother had been so circumspect about the beautiful woman I had seen. And then the woman began to walk toward me with her arms outstretched, beckoning me toward her. She sang to me in a gutteral tone.

> As the Goddess will prevail,
> Bring light to the great halls of Avalon—
> Island of flame,
> The Queens go up the mountain Tor,
> The gateway of yore.
> The elves have let us pass.
> The evil one hangs upon my spear—
> No sorcerer elf escapes a woman of wings,
> Anne's soul and spirit to you I bring.

Shakily, I stood up from my chair. The area around my navel ached. As I walked toward her, she became older and older with each step I took. It was both fascinating and horrifying, as if I were watching someone age forty or fifty years right before my eyes.

"The elves make repentance at the halls of Derwenydd," she said.

Then suddenly came a moan from Anne, and my eyes left Grandmother's face to look down at her. We all knelt down and put our arms under and around her. She began to flail around on the floor. I was frightened and did not know what to do. I looked up at the woman who had been walking toward me and saw the face of Grandmother intently looking down into Anne's eyes. She placed her hands on either side of her head, then brushed carefully over her face with a slapping sound one of the feathers from her cloak. It was a long eagle feather tipped in white. She crooned to Anne as if she were crooning to a baby. And this time in English she asked the spirit to move back into her body. She pressed down on her stomach with the heels of both hands, pushing hard. Anne lurched and took a deep breath, as if she had been choking, unable to get any air. Grandmother repeated this until Anne was breathing normally.

I watched as the color came back into Anne's cheeks. I watched as the perspiration disappeared from her face. I watched with disbelief and excitement and, finally, gratitude as she opened her eyes and looked up at us as if she were awakening from a long night's sleep. As she looked around at the falcons on their perches and the owl's head hanging down over Grandmother's forehead, the candles burning and the air thick with incense smoke, she realized that something terrible had happened to her. Tears filled her eyes, and she held out her arms to Grandmother, who picked her up in her arms like a young child. The four of us helped to wrap her in her bedding and carry her back to her bedchamber.

Moments later she was sitting up in bed with a bright look of health on her face as if nothing at all had happened. We all sat around her laughing and talking all at the same time. Grandmother had put away her ceremonial feathers and cloaks. Quickly, Charles and Alice had taken away the altar, and everything was put away out of view, except for the candles that continued to burn in Anne's room.

We talked about what had happened. Grandmother explained to Anne that she had had to make a journey into the spirit world.

"What did I do, Grandmother, to dishonor the elves? I do not understand how this could have happened," Anne said, looking wide-eyed at Grandmother.

"Not long ago, Anne, you met your male friend in one of the sacred caves, and you did not leave food for the elves, because you did not want him to know you followed the way of Wyrrd. You did not want him to know about your sacred life. You dishonored the elves, and you *know* that you dishonored them."

Anne bowed her head, blushing violently. Charles and Alice and I exchanged knowing looks.

"I beg forgiveness of all of you," Anne said. "I have frightened all of you, and I have made you go to much trouble to save me. I promise, with all that is sacred within me, that I will never transgress in such a way again."

Grandmother looked at her very sternly. "Anne, it will take you a year to mend what you have done. You must go to the cave; first you must gather running water from the falls at Derwenydd, and you must take all the herbs that I will teach you about in the next few days. You offer the herbs along with food for the elves, and you must sing sacred chants to them and make a circle. You must do this at every new moon for the rest of the year. It is important that you never forget, and if something happens and you cannot go, you must let me know and I will do it for you. Otherwise, you will lose your soul forever."

After a moment of silence, I asked, "What happened when you went to the land of the dead?"

"I found Anne's guardians. They were just on the other side of the gateway. I went to them and I asked if I could pass, and they said no. They said that what Anne had done was a test, and it had to do with a past lifetime. They wanted her to pay for what she had done."

"What had she done, Grandmother?" I asked.

"The young man she brought to the cave had been her husband in another life, and she had left him for another man."

Anne looked at Grandmother, shocked. "You mean that I have known him in another life?" She shook her head. "You know, I knew that. There was a bond between us. I knew that there had to be more than just this life experience between us," she said.

"Yes," Grandmother said. "It is true. Sometimes what we have done in other lifetimes comes back to haunt us. You nearly died, my child. It was so close; it was the closest I have ever seen someone come to losing her soul forever. I could barely convince the guardians to let me pass. I had to make much sacrifice to them."

"What did you have to sacrifice?" Anne asked.

"I, too, will have to go to the cave. I, too, will have to make offerings. Do not be concerned, my child. That is part of my work, and I am happy to do it. But never again will you do such a thing without letting me know first. If you had told me, I could have been ready for this and I could have helped you. I do not want anything to happen to you."

Grandmother kissed Anne on the forehead. "It is being healed, my child. You sleep now. You have been through quite an ordeal."

"And so have you," Alice said, getting up and putting her arms around Grandmother.

Charles and Alice and I gathered around Grandmother and hugged and kissed her. Grandmother turned to me and said, "Well, Catherine, did you enjoy the performance?"

I nodded my head. "Yes, it was an extraordinary event. I have learned, tonight, many new things."

"You go to sleep now, Catherine, and tomorrow we will discuss everything that you saw. And I will explain what you do not understand. I will help you understand my journey into the spirit world. Thank you for helping me in my ceremony. Good night," she said, giving me a hug.

I looked toward Alice.

"We will talk again soon when I see you in the other world. Just pretend that this never happened. We have a secret now between us. It is good. It means that we are sisters." She winked at me.

Then I turned to Charles. I am sure that I blushed. He winked at me.

"We too have a secret between us," he said cocking his head to one side.

I was speechless. I wanted to say so much to him, and I could say nothing. I left the room wondering if I would ever see him again.

CHAPTER · 17

MASQUERADE
OF A
LIGHT BEING

ON A MORNING NOT long after that night I awoke to my mother opening the draperies that hung over my windows, letting a flood of light into my room.

"Good morning, daughter," she said, coming over to sit beside me on the bed.

"Good morning, Mother," I said, wiping the sleep out of my eyes and blinking in the sudden light. I sat up on my pillow.

"It will be May soon, Catherine, and we will be having our annual masked ball. I want to know what you would like to wear. Perhaps this year you could have a new dress."

"Oh, Mother, that will be wonderful. What do you think I should go as?" I asked excitedly.

"You could go as a fairy princess," she said, wiping the strands of hair away from my forehead with her perfumed fingers.

"I know. Perhaps I could go as the Queen of the Elves," I said.

"The Queen of the Elves?" Mother looked at me questioningly and then added, "I did not know there was a Queen of the Elves. What an uncommon idea."

I was thinking back to Anne, and I thought perhaps if I went as the Queen of the Elves, it would be my way of honoring the elves. Even though this ball would be part of another world, I was sure the elves would know of the celebration, and I would do my own little ceremony before coming downstairs to the dance.

My mother got up from the bed and began walking around examining the tables for dust and looking at the tapestries that hung on the walls.

"Yes, Catherine, what a good idea. I will go to the seamstress this morning and I will tell her what you want. We will come up with something quite unusual." Mother came over and kissed me on the forehead and left the room.

I spent that day and the next week helping to prepare for the ball. I knew that Grandmother would understand. I knew that working now would leave days at week's end free for my work with her. I practiced easing my luminous fibers and moving my astral body up to the ceiling every night, exploring the rest of my home while everybody slept. I was actually getting quite good at it, and I knew that Grandmother would be very happy with the work that I had done.

Before I knew it, the day of the masked ball had arrived. The stone house and compound that I called home on the hill near Collingham's lake was alive with preparation. The candles were lit, and as darkness fell, guests began to arrive, their horses and carriages clattering up the drive and into the courtyard.

My dress was pink satin, edged with magnificent French lace around the edge of the skirt. It floated out around me like a pink cloud, and the mask, which was on a stick so I could hold it up to my eyes, was just properly alluring for a girl of my age. My mane of hair had been done up in a mass of ringlets that cascaded down to my shoulders. I knew that I looked wonderful, and I was very excited. I felt as though I were going to my first party.

I knew that the Lady of Glastonbury and her family would be there, and I could not wait to see them. But they were late arriving, and it was not until well into the evening that they made their entrance. There were several people in her family — her daughters, her husband. I looked carefully as they entered the great ballroom, and then I saw him. It did not look like Charles, but I knew that it had to be him.

He was dressed as a dashing swordsman in a blue velvet cape and a wonderful hat with a huge plume that bobbed up and down as he moved. I was so happy to see him I could scarcely breathe. When he came over to me and bowed gracefully at my feet, he looked up over the black ribbon mask that he wore across his eyes and smiled at me disarmingly. My mother did not notice the exchange between us; she was busy with her guests.

Alice took my hand, squeezed it knowingly, and winked at me. She went off with her husband to see other people, and Charles and I were left standing together. As the music began, he asked me to dance. He held my hands firmly in his and led me out onto the dance floor. It was thronged with an extraordinary gathering of people. We danced between ring-tailed cats and princes and kings and witches and strange big birds fashioned out of satin and lace and pieces of striped cotton. It was as if we were in a dream, as if we had moved onto another planet full of strange and wonderful creatures the likes of which I had never seen before. I wished I could have shared this with Grandmother. She would have enjoyed it so much.

Then I lost all perception of the people swirling around me. All I could think of or be aware of was this young man who was holding me so gently in his arms. He danced beautifully, and it was easy for me to follow every step. At one point he held me to his chest as we swirled around to miss another pair of dancers. I thought my heart would burst with the touch of him. I looked up into his handsome face.

"Would you mind taking me outside? I think I need to breathe fresh air," I said.

"Yes, of course, Catherine. Come. Follow me."

He held my hand and led me off the dance floor through the crush of people, outside through the tall doors to the balcony overlooking the garden. We sat there in the moonlight saying nothing for some time. He took his mask off and looked at me carefully, making me nervous. I could find nothing at all to say.

"You are so beautiful, Catherine," he finally said. I blushed, and looked down at the ground, unable to unlock my voice.

"There is something that you must know about me," Charles said very seriously. He reached out and held my hand, and he said, "Look at me, please. This is very important. I do not want to mislead you, Catherine."

I looked at him sharply, listening to his words. "Go ahead, Charles. What is it you have to say to me?"

"I want you to know that I think you are one of the most beautiful young women I have ever met."

I started to blush again, and he said, "No, no. Do not be shy. What I have to say is truthful and important. Look at me," he demanded. I looked back into his eyes, hardly able to bear it. "I want you to know that I am a wizard. I have been working with the forces that be, for a very long time, perhaps as long as Grandmother."

He let the words settle in as my eyes widened. I shook my head. "But Charles, that cannot be. You are so young. You are Alice's son. What are you talking about?"

"As we get to know each other, Catherine, you will learn many things, many things that now are not appropriate to tell you. But try to understand. I do not want us to misunderstand each other."

"What do you mean, Charles?"

"I am going to tell you something very directly." He paused for a moment, then he held my gaze. "I am a wizard. I am a man of power in the ancient way of Wyrrd. To do the work that I must do on this earth, I can never be married. I could never ask you to be my wife."

I was stunned. I thought to myself—Can he read my mind? Does he know how deeply in love with him I am? He looked into my eyes and placed the back of his hand against my cheek.

"Catherine, I feel many of the things that you feel. And yes, I know what is in your mind, and one day you will know what is in my mind."

"But why can you never marry?" I asked.

"To say it in the simplest way," he said, settling himself in his chair, "is to say that to become attached to another human being, to become involved in the responsibilities of a family, of a wife and children, would take too much time away from what I am here to do. I have known from the time I was born that I am here to do certain things. But one thing I cannot do is marry. I want you to know that, because I do not want you to be hurt. All of this is very new to you, and I am sure that you are going to feel cheated, betrayed. I do not want you to feel that. I want you to know that I am your friend and will remain your friend, but that I can never marry you or anyone else. If I were able to marry, it would be you."

Tears stung my eyelids. I fought desperately to keep from crying. "How is it that we know all this so soon? Since you are giving me the gift of being so honest with me, I will tell you that the moment I saw you I fell deeply in love with you," I said.

"We know these things because, whether you believe it or not, we have been together in many lifetimes. One day, not in this lifetime but in another that is soon to come, I will come to you on a black stallion. I will carry you away and become your spirit husband. But in this lifetime we have much work to do. We must be careful, you and I, because to lose each other would be a tragedy. To lose ourselves in each other would also be a tragedy."

"But, Charles, why would that be so terrible? It is what everyone wants — to feel like this. I thought I would never feel like this."

"There is nothing wrong with the way you feel. You may meet someone that you choose to marry. It would be wonderful for you to be married in this lifetime, but it is not good for me. It would take my power. It is one of the agreements I made with my teachers long ago, and it is an agreement that I must honor, that I cannot ignore. It is something that we cannot even discuss after this moment. You must understand clearly. For us to be friends you must look at me as your brother and not as your lover. It is the way of Wyrrd. There is nothing we can do. We are born and we die with a destiny. You have yours, and I have mine. Within our spirit circle, Catherine, we will work together, but we cannot have each other, not this time."

He reached out his arms and he held me, really held me, for the first time — and perhaps for the last time. Then he tilted up my chin with his fingers and kissed me gently on the lips. It was the first time I had ever been kissed by a man. As I watched him turn and walk away, I knew that it would be the last time in this lifetime I would be kissed, because I knew that I would love him always.

. . .

That night and the next several days I could not leave my bed. In my grief, I did not want to live. My parents would come in and tend to me. It was as if I were in a trance. I could not awaken, and I could not really sleep. I felt that my heart had been crushed. I did not know how to cope with my feelings. I did not know how I was going to survive.

Days went by. I could not eat, and I was becoming dangerously ill. My parents were at their wits' end. They could not understand what was the matter with me. Of course, I did not tell them.

Then one afternoon, Alice came to visit me. My mother ushered her in, and she was surprised—I could see it on her face—that Alice had come to see me. Alice explained that she felt a special kinship with me. She thought that perhaps she could help. She asked my mother to leave the room. When Mother had gone, she closed the door and locked it then came over and sat on my bed. I put my arms around her and sobbed on her shoulder. I sobbed and sobbed until I could not cry any longer. She laid me back on the pillows and shook her head.

"My child, I know how you feel. I am sure you believe that no one has ever felt the anguish you are feeling now, but believe me, I do understand. I am a woman of Wyrrd like Grandmother, because I met such a man as Charles when I too was a young girl."

"You mean, you met someone as handsome as Charles and as wonderful as he? I cannot imagine that another man like him has ever lived."

"Yes, Catherine, I did, and I had to get over him, just as you must. Later I met my husband, and I love him very much. We were married, and my life went on."

"But, Alice, once you are in love, how can you ever fall in love with someone else?"

"Well, just imagine, Catherine; if something happened to Charles, if he were killed, you would have to go on with your life. There would be nothing else to do."

"But Alice, I do not know how. I do not know how to live past this moment. I wish I were dead. I really do not want to live without him. I feel as if my soul is gone. There is no life inside me."

Alice reached out and caressed my forehead. "You are so beautiful, Catherine. You must understand that the work you are doing with Grandmother and with the rest of us is more important than anything else. It is more important than your love for Charles or his for you."

"But I do not believe that, Alice. I think that they are equally important."

"That's true, Catherine. Love for other human beings is the reason we do our work at all. We care about the balance of this magnificent earth we live on. We care about preserving her magic and her power. There are few people in the world that can do what we can. There are few who can commit this knowledge to memory and pass it on to our apprentices and our daughters and sons. Because of that, we have to put knowledge first. We are the keepers of the wisdom of Wyrrd, and that is a great and extraordinary responsibility. You know that, Catherine. You know that you have been born to this destiny. You knew it from the very beginning. I have always seen this destiny in you, but no one can tell you about it. You have to find it for yourself, or I would have been working with you years ago. It took you a while, but that is fine. We all need to come to it in our own time. There are certain people in every time who feel this destiny and are drawn to the truth. Most people ignore their inner need to search for truth. They become distracted, and they live differently than you and I and Charles."

"Oh, Alice, there is so much that I do not understand. I am so glad that you came here to speak to me. I am sure I would have died if you had not."

Alice looked at me for several minutes, stroking my hand. "And have you not thought of Grandmother in this time that you have been in bed?"

"Oh yes, Alice, I have, and I am so ashamed. I cannot believe that I am as weak as I am. But I must tell you that all I care about at this moment is Charles. I do care about Grandmother, and about my family, but I feel possessed, as if I have lost my soul to Charles. I do not know how else to explain it, even though I know that I sound stupid and childish."

"Grandmother has been very worried about you, my child. She wants you to go see her as soon as you can. It is important that you do so. Grandmother is a great woman, and she will help you to find strength to live again. She will help you to understand what is happening to you. I know that it is very difficult for you. We are all very anxious that you re-cover and find your way. I want you to know that I love you, Catherine, and Charles loves you. He is so sorry that you are in pain and wants you to know he is in pain as well. It is easier for him, because he has been in this work so much longer than you have. He understands more clearly what his destiny is. Let him help you; let us all help you to grow from this experience. I leave you with my blessings, and I leave you with my love. We will see you before the moon is full again." Alice leaned over and kissed me on the forehead. "Go to see Grandmother as quickly as you can," she said as she left my room.

The next morning I woke up feeling a little bit stronger. I got dressed as quickly as I could. I was incredibly weak. I went down the back stairs and out to the stable, where James saddled my horse for me, my beautiful horse that I had not seen in days. I had missed him. I kissed him on the nose; he seemed excited that I had come to ride him. He snorted and pawed the ground as James helped me into the saddle. I hoped that I would make it to Grandmother's without falling off.

"You look very pale, Miss Catherine," James said, with great concern.

"I will be fine, James. If Mother asks after me, tell her that I am fine, that I just wanted to go out and be by myself for a while. I will return be-fore dark."

A short time later I was sitting in Grandmother's stone cottage. She was fixing me a very special herbal drink that did not smell good.

"What is this, Grandmother? It smells very strange."

"It will help you, my child," Grandmother said. "I am very glad to see you, Catherine. I have been very concerned. I know what you have been going through, and I want to help you."

"Oh, Grandmother, how can anyone understand? It is so awful to love someone and know that you can never have him. How could this have happened to me? Nothing ever works out right."

"The ways of Wyrrd are very strange. The ways of power ask a great deal of us. When these ways are new to us, it is even more difficult. I wish that I could reach into your heart and make you see how important this work is."

Grandmother sat down in front of me and handed me a piece of pie that she had made from the fruit-bearing trees in her garden. I took a bite. It tasted so good. I sipped some more of the strange smelling drink. I was beginning to feel better with every sip that I took.

"Grandmother, I feel as if my soul is gone. I feel like a tent with the stakes removed. I feel as though I have lost my form. I do not know how else to describe it. I love Charles so deeply. I feel as if I have known him all my life, as if he knows every secret hidden within my heart. And I feel I know his heart as well. How can that possibly be? I do not know him, not really."

"It is only possible because you do know him. You just do not remember."

"What do you mean, Grandmother?"

"I mean that you have known him in many lifetimes. You have worked together before."

"Oh, Grandmother, I do not know if I care about having worked together. I just want to be with him. I want to be with him, and I want to understand this," I said, realizing that I was disconnected and not really paying attention to what Grandmother was trying to say to me.

She grabbed my shoulders and shook me gently. "Catherine, you must listen to me."

"If Charles has been working with you for so long, why have I not met him before?" I asked.

"We had to wait until you were strong enough, but when Anne became so ill, she needed him. We knew that when the two of you came together again, you would instantly fall in love. It has happened before, and it will happen in other lifetimes. You have been together before. When are you going to hear me? In this lifetime you are not destined to be married to each other. You can work together and be friends, but you must find the place inside you where you understand this more clearly. You cannot possess each other in this lifetime," Grandmother said, intense with worry and concern.

"Grandmother, I am hearing your words, but they are not sinking in. I am in a glass box, and you are on the outside. I see you talking, but I cannot really hear you."

"You have lost your soul. You have lost it, not because Charles has taken it from you, but because you have willingly given it away. Women so often give away their power. That seems to be the instinct of man and woman when they fall in love. They give away their power to each other, which is a sure sign that they are not truly ready to be in love. If you can remain strong with Charles, if you can learn to hold your power and he can hold his, then you will be ready for each other. Then you will have a true marriage in the way of Wyrrd. That is what we call a marriage of power, and it is one of the strongest connections between human beings. But you are not ready for this yet, Catherine."

"How do you know I am not ready for it?" I said, almost in tears.

Grandmother looked at me. She could not help but smile a little. "Because you have lost your soul already. If you had been able to meet him and not lose your soul, then perhaps it would have been different."

"Are you saying to me, Grandmother, that I failed a test?"

"It was a test of power, not a test that we as human beings set for you."

"I do not understand, Grandmother."

"What I am saying is that it was already written. It was written by the Goddess Mother that you would meet in this lifetime and would not be able to have each other, because neither of you is ready."

"But I can be ready. Just teach me, and I will become ready in this lifetime."

Grandmother heaved a sigh and took a bite of pie. "The first thing we must do, Catherine, is get you your spirit back before you become truly ill. Your spirit shield is wandering on its way to the land of the dead, and we must regain her."

"How do we do that, Grandmother?" I was suddenly frightened. "Do you mean that my spirit is actually gone? Is that why I feel so terribly strange, why I cannot really hear you? I am having trouble seeing you. And I feel so faint."

"Yes, Catherine, that is why."

"But who has taken it?" I asked, as if I had not heard all the things she had just been saying to me.

"I think you know the answer to that, my child. I want you to rest, and we will do a ceremony tomorrow night to regain your spirit shield."

"What kind of ceremony, Grandmother? Is this what happened to Anne? What will I have to do?"

"You will be guided," Grandmother said. "We will do everything. This is similar to what happened to Anne, but it involves your spirit, not your soul. You can live through this, but Anne was close to death. You, however, could lose your will to live."

"How can this be happening?" I moaned.

"Your spirit shield is spinning through space like a falling star. It could explode, and you could lose all the precious wisdom that you have gained. It could be stolen by anyone who has the strength to reach out and take it. That is how people live off the power of someone else. If Charles were a dark magician, he would take your spirit shield and call it his own. But he wants only to restore your shield and make it stronger. He is a true wizard. He knows that within your power lives his own."

"Who will be at the ceremony?" I asked.

"Catherine, do not bother yourself with these things. Come. I want you to rest. You do not look well."

"But I am supposed to be home by dark," I said.

"You go home now and rest," Grandmother said. "Come back, and I promise you, your life will begin anew, and you will feel better. I do not want anyone at your home to be alarmed. You go home now and take care, my child. All will be well."

"Will Charles be here when I get back?" I asked.

"Yes. He will have to help us find your spirit shield."

I was overjoyed to think that I would be able to see his face once again at least.

"I will be back, Grandmother. I will be back as early tomorrow as I can get here."

Grandmother gave me a kiss on the forehead as I left her house.

CHAPTER · 18

RETURN
OF
WINDHORSE

I FELL ASLEEP THAT NIGHT crying and feeling so weak that I did not know whether I could get up and go to the ceremony the next day at Grandmother's. All I could do was try. But instead of waking up the next morning in my bed in England, I woke up in the Dreamlodge in Manitoba. Ruby and Agnes were both shaking me, and even in my physical body I was extremely weak. I felt a lack of energy, a lack of interest. I was in an extreme state of depression.

"Great Spirit, when will we ever get you to hold your power!" Ruby said, clucking her tongue.

Agnes said nothing. She removed the necklace and kept rubbing her hands up and down my arms vigorously. Her eyes betrayed her concern. I had never seen either of the women moving in such an agitated manner, rubbing my feet, my legs, and my arms trying to awaken me. I didn't want to wake up. I wanted to move back into sleep in hope that I could find my way to Grandmother's house. Again and again I would close my eyes. Agnes and Ruby would pound on me, knead my body with their fingers, pinch me. Finally, as I started to swoon, they lifted me up off the sheepskins and carried me between them outside and dunked me in the creek. The water was icy cold, and I shrieked, suddenly furious with both of them.

"You wake up, and you wake up now!" Agnes said, shaking my shoulders and slapping me across both cheeks until my skin smarted under her palm.

"I'm awake, damnit, I'm awake," I growled.

I sat down on the bank of the creek and hoped that I would get pneumonia and die. There was nothing in me that seemed to want to live. The newly chilled blood was coursing through my veins. It occurred to me that I was behaving strangely.

"What is the matter with me?" I slurred through the foggy imprint of my mind.

"What's the matter with you is that you have allowed your power to be stolen." They both glared at me.

"How can my power have been stolen?" I protested, almost under my breath.

"It can be stolen by someone a little smarter than you," Ruby said as she placed a blanket around my shoulders and rubbed my back vigorously.

"Look at me," she said. "Tell me what has happened to you," she ordered.

"Why is it so important?" I asked.

"Because, you silly girl, if we do not hear what has happened to you, we cannot help you. You are going to pass out very shortly. You will not have the strength to stay awake, and when you move into the other world, I want to be able to help you. We cannot follow you if we do not know what is happening."

"What do you mean I'm going to pass out?"

"Exactly what I said," Agnes stated. "But you listen to me. I don't know what has happened, but I want you to tell me and I want you to tell me now. So go ahead," she demanded, pounding her fist on her knee.

I stuttered for several minutes, not knowing even where to begin, and finally I just blurted it out. I was too tired to try to form the words into coherent thoughts.

"I met a wizard," I said.

Ruby looked at me and rolled her eyes, looking at the sky and shaking her head.

"Oh, no," she said. "Don't tell me."

"Don't tell you what?" I said.

In unison the old women looked at me and said, "Don't tell us that you have fallen in love."

"Yes," I said in a tiny voice. "What's wrong with that?" I asked.

Then it all came back to me like a rush of river water through an open dike. Thoughts of Charles filled my mind as if he were someone on this present physical plane. My eyelids started to droop again. I wanted to go back into sleep. Together Agnes and Ruby put me back in the river, and this time they held me down until I fought for air.

"Okay, okay," I said as they dragged me back onto the river bank. "I get the message. I get the message, all right? I understand that something is wrong. I will try to be more disciplined. Okay? Just leave me alone for a minute. Let me walk around."

I grabbed the old blue Pendleton blanket, wrapped it around me closely, and tried to get to my feet. They both helped me. I tried to take a step and crumbled in the dirt. I couldn't believe I was so weak. It scared me. I tried to wake up even further, shaking my head, and realized that I was in real trouble. I had always had tremendous endurance. No matter what had happened to me, I had always been able to gain my balance if I tried and if I paid attention. Now I realized that my body was not responding. Something was wrong. I felt completely different than I had ever felt in my life. I allowed Agnes and Ruby to help me into the cabin. They sat me down in a chair and started firing questions at me as they poured tea down me, very strong tea, in hopes that the caffeine would perhaps revive me a little. Agnes and Ruby sat across from me, each holding one of my hands. Agnes looked at me with more intensity than I had ever seen, with her face turned to the side, so she was looking at me through her left eye.

"There is nothing wrong with falling in love, Lynn, but the person you have fallen in love with has taken your spirit. There is something wrong with that. That doesn't usually happen," Agnes said, "now, does it?"

"No, it doesn't," I said to Agnes. "Actually he hasn't taken my spirit; I have given it to him."

"Well, it doesn't surprise me," Ruby said. "Who is this man anyway, this wizard?"

"His name is Charles of Glastonbury. He is the son of Lady Alice of Glastonbury. They are friends of my family—I guess, of Catherine's family," I said, getting confused.

Agnes and Ruby looked at each other. Agnes took a deep sigh and looked back at me, and she said, "We were afraid of this."

I looked at her. "Are you saying that you know about Charles, that you knew that this was going to happen?"

"My child, there is much that you do not understand yet."

I stood up from the chair with enormous effort, gathered what was left of my strength, and screamed at the top of my lungs. "Well, don't you think it's about time you tell me before I die on you?"

I sat down and collapsed, no more strength left in my body. Nobody said anything for a moment. I glared at Agnes and then Ruby.

"You have put me in enormous danger. You have not told me something that I should have known to prepare myself had I known that I was going to meet someone that I would fall this deeply in love with. Doesn't it occur to you that perhaps I could have been a little prepared?" I asked.

"You can never tell someone about an experience that she is going to have. You can never tell her how to behave or how not to behave, because then you would be cheating her of that experience. How were we to know that you would give away your spirit to this wizard man? We knew that you would like him. We were hoping that he could become your partner, that you could work equally together, stand strongly under the shade of one tree, each of you separate and powerful. We did not imagine that you would lose yourself to him in this way," Agnes said, Ruby nodding her agreement.

"Well, did it ever occur to you that I am a very young girl in this experience and I don't know very much? I am not the person sitting here, and I must tell you that even if I were the person sitting here, I would have been in love with him. He is everything I have ever dreamed of in a man."

"You said that about Red Dog, too, don't forget," Agnes said.

"Yes, but this is different," I said.

"Oh, I see. And how is it different?" Ruby asked.

"It's different, because this is of my choosing. I am not under a spell," I said.

"And how do you know that?" Agnes asked. "How do you know this man is not also living off your energy and your heat? How do you know that he hasn't maneuvered you into a position and has actually stolen your soul?" Agnes asked with a very serious expression on her face.

"I know, because I went to see Grandmother, and she told me that in my lack of experience and power I had given away to him."

"How long have you known him?" Agnes asked.

"I have only known him, or I should say Catherine has only known him, well, she's only seen him a couple of times actually. But she fell in love with him the moment he came in the room."

"Oh, I see," Ruby said. "You've had a chance to develop a long and meaningful relationship. I can see why this is so serious." She shook her head with disgust.

"I believe in love at first sight," I said with great seriousness. "I really mean it," I said.

For the first time Agnes looked at me with compassion. "Yes, it is true, Lynn. There is such a thing as love at first sight, and I know that the Catherine in you is in great, great pain. I understand it. I felt that way once in my life also. So Ruby, you leave her alone. I know how she feels," Agnes said, patting the back of my hand.

"Why does he have to be a wizard? I don't understand why he can't marry in this lifetime," I said.

"How do I explain this to you, Lynn? This life is not as it seems. You must be learning that by living your life as Catherine so many centuries ago as if it were today. You must be beginning to see that this earth truly is a schoolhouse, that we have come here to become enlightened, and it really is all there is. Our relationships, our families, our children are simply mirrors. I've told you this so many times, but it needs saying again, particularly when you are in such depth of pain. You must understand with your whole being that you are a teacher, that you are being trained by a consciousness beyond your imagination. And you must remember that you have made a bid for power centuries ago, and power has come to you. One way power has come to you is through this young man, Charles the Wizard of Glastonbury. He also is not as he seems. Charles is a good man, and I am sure that he does not mean to hurt you."

"Oh yes, Agnes, he told me that. He told me right away who he was, and he told me that he could not marry in that lifetime, that he did not want to hurt me. But it was too late; I had already fallen for him."

"Has he asked you to work with him?" Ruby asked.

"Yes, he said he hoped that we could work together in that lifetime. He also told me that he would come to me — "

I stopped. I suddenly remembered something he had said to me, or rather, to Catherine.

"What is the matter?" Agnes said, watching me falter.

"I remember that he said to Catherine that he would come to her on a black stallion and that he would become her spirit husband in another life and that I should remember him, or that Catherine should remember him. It is hard for me. I can't remember who I am sometimes. I don't know if I am Catherine or Lynn."

"It is all right, Lynn. Don't worry about it. What I need is some information."

"Oh, my God, Agnes. He's Windhorse, isn't he?" I remembered my experience in the Valley of Luktang in Tibet when I had met Windhorse, my spirit husband, and we had married in a Dreamtime ceremony.

Agnes looked at me and smiled.

"And you knew that, didn't you, Agnes? Because you told me in Nepal that something very wonderful was going to happen to me. That's what you meant. You described this experience. Now I remember."

Ruby reached across the table and took hold of my hand.

"It would help now, Lynn, if you went to Windhorse. Do your ceremony in the Dreamlodge, and ask him to come to you. Talk to him. You will realize the extraordinary gift that Windhorse is to you. You have loved him for a very long time."

Tears welled up in my eyes as I realized that he was actually with me and would always be with me.

"But, Ruby, is it true? He is Charles, isn't he? And you both knew it. Oh, my God, I don't know if I even know where to put this experience. I'm not sure I can handle it."

"Why is there something to handle?" Agnes said. "All there is, is the pure beauty of truth. It is the truth that we are in fact all one, that the duality of this life is simply an illusion. What is all of this wisdom and all of this work and all of this struggle but the Great Spirit creating a way for us to find our way home? You are walking down the trail toward home. Never forget that. Charles, or Windhorse, is part of that march. He is part of your own totality. He is a reflection of the warrior that lives inside you. We are all looking for that warrior or warrioress that dwells within us. A man looks for his warrioress, and a woman looks for her warrior. And when she finds him, she mates with him. She mates with him in the physical, and she mates with him in spirit. When she can accomplish that, she becomes whole. That is why, in a sense, your journey to the Valley of Luktang and your meeting with Windhorse and the Book of the Child was the end of your first hoop of learning. It was the closure on your first series of shaman endeavors. Now you are walking the second hoop, and that second hoop is dealing with what has brought you to this lifetime. And what has brought you here partly is your work with Charles the Wizard of Glastonbury and many others, certainly Grandmother. But you will learn that later. The most important thing now is that you go into the Dreamlodge before it is too late, and let him come to you. When you go back to be with Grandmother, try with all your heart to retain this memory. It will be very vague, but perhaps this experience will give you strength to give Charles and Catherine a way to their higher purpose. That will be a great learning for you and a great victory for everyone in the Sisterhood.

"Come. Now we will take you back to the Dreamlodge. We will give you something to eat and help you on your way."

I sat back in the chair as they brought biscuits and smoked fish. The thought of eating made me gag, but I got it down anyway in hopes that it would give me strength. It seemed to give me a little, and on my way back to the Dreamlodge, I felt a little stronger.

The two women did a ceremony around the outside of the lodge. After they had laid me down on the sheep skins, they relit the candles and the lanterns and stoked the fire so it was pleasantly warm. It was only a few minutes before I was in deep sleep.

. . .

I did the ceremony in the Dreamtime that I always do to bring in Windhorse. Before I knew it, I was in a high valley in the Himalayas, a small lush valley. I was sitting in front of the fire in the small stone house that belonged to Windhorse. I could hear his stallion whinnying outside. As I looked into his face, it all became clear to me. He smiled at me in his boyish way, sitting there proud and powerful. He wore a yellow, hand-woven shirt and black boots, a belt with a silver buckle around his waist, and a scarf made of many colors around his neck. His eyes sparkled with the light from the fire. There was tremendous kindness in his eyes and around his mouth.

"So you are in trouble again," he said, laughing. He reached out to hold my hand. "When will you remember that we are part of each other?" he asked.

I trembled as he took my hand. He gathered me into his arms and held me for a long time as he would have held a child. All the tension and the pain and the longing drained out of my body as if he were absorbing it like a sponge. He stroked my hair with his hands and told me that everything would be all right. I believed him, because I knew it was true. When I looked into his face, I shook my head.

"How could I not have recognized you?" I asked. "How could I be so stupid?"

"It was the first time that you have seen me incarnate in the physical. It was the first time that you traveled into your past history, and that is a very difficult thing. You are going to be a wizard yourself," he said, "one of these days."

We talked about Catherine; we talked about me; and we talked about the difficulties of our chosen path. We talked about how difficult it was to carry on a normal life and still remain deeply rooted in the mysteries. He talked to me some about what he was doing, about the difficulties in Tibet these days and how difficult it was to hide the chosen knowledge.

"We are both on the same path, aren't we?" I said. "We are just doing it differently than most people."

"Yes," he said. "It is important to remember that whatever I do is still part of you. Whatever you do is still part of me."

"Thank you so much for reminding me of that and for reminding me that we are together."

He took my face in his hands.

"Never forget who you are," he said.

With that he picked a necklace up off the table and placed it around my neck. I looked at it, held it, and ran my fingers over the circle with the crosses engraved with the four directions. I gasped as I recognized the amulet that had been hanging over my altar in the Dreamlodge.

"That is another wedding present I had for you," he said. "I think it is appropriate that you wear it now."

He held me in his arms. Suddenly a burst of light filled the room. I closed my eyes as my entire body shook. I felt the energy of the universe rumble through me. I felt my spirit spiral inside my body, then shoot out the top of my head. Before I knew it, I was back on my sheepskins looking at the top of the Dreamlodge and Agnes and Ruby. They looked down at me questioningly.

I smiled. "Yes, I was with him. Don't worry. I understand now."

I took a deep breath, closed my eyes again, and fell back into a deep sleep.

. . .

When I awoke next morning, as Catherine, I still felt very ill, but the pain had lessened. I knew something had happened, but I had no idea what it was. I had no memory of Windhorse. I had no memory of my spirit husband or of Agnes and Ruby or of any other lifetime. I put on my clothes and went to ask my parents if I could visit my friend Anne for a few days. They were so overjoyed to see me feeling better that they didn't even ask me any questions. I packed a small bag and went down to the stables. My father helped me on my horse, said good-bye to me with a kiss, and told me to be careful.

By the time I arrived at Grandmother's, I was desperately weak, just managing to stay on my horse. She helped me down and into the cottage. I sat down with her gratefully at the table.

"What is it, my child? You have changed, Catherine. What is happening?"

"I cannot explain it, Grandmother, except that I feel better. I know that I am still ill and I still agonize for Charles, but I feel better somehow. I feel that I am going to understand this. I still cannot really imagine my life without him, but I think perhaps it will be all right. I do not really know why I say this."

I knew that my voice was very tiny and I had half the energy I normally did, but I knew I also had grown somehow.

Grandmother came over and felt my forehead. She said, "It is very dangerous what has happened to you, Catherine, and I understand your pain. We are here to help you. We will try not to let anything happen to you."

It was the first time I had heard Grandmother use the word *try*.

"Is it possible I might not recover my spirit shield?" I was alarmed.

"There *is* that possibility. I cannot lie to you," Grandmother said. "But I think that you are going to be better very quickly," she said, looking deep into my eyes. "I think something has happened to you. Do not worry now. I want you to go to bed; tonight we will do the ceremony."

"When will Charles be here?" I asked.

"At nightfall. I do not want you to stay up any longer. I am afraid you are going to be too weak."

"Will I be able to see him?" I asked.

"Oh, yes." Grandmother nodded her head. "I am going to gather herbs now. There are many things I need to do to prepare for this ceremony."

"Is Alice coming too?" I asked.

"Yes, and some others."

"Some others?" I said.

"Yes," Grandmother answered. "But do not concern yourself. It is important that you do not worry."

"There's one thing that I must do," I said.

"And what is that?"

"I must speak with Charles."

"You may do so after the ceremony," she said, "but not before. This is important."

"All right, Grandmother. I understand," and I got up and walked into the bedchamber.

CHAPTER · 19

THE
LABYRINTH

I LAY IN BED AT Grandmother's house, moving in and out of fitful sleep. Sometimes I would wake with a fever, my face and body soaking wet. Then I would wake and feel as if I were getting better, and I would lie there and listen to the sounds of the old stone house and of Grandmother preparing for the ceremony that night. I thought of Grandmother's words and what she had said about losing my spirit. It sounded to me very much like Anne's soul being stolen by the elves. If one loses one's soul, doesn't that mean one is dead? I pondered the difference between my spirit and my soul.

A shiver of fear ran down my spine as I realized that I felt my life force waning. I had half the energy — or even less — that I had had a few days before. I had heard people talk about that in the past — when someone became very ill, they said that person's spirit was being stolen by a dwarf or an elf. What had really happened was that the soul had abandoned the body and allowed a disease to come in that could kill the person. I realized I was in danger of dying. It was as if my body were rallying every force that it could, every force available to it, to ward off any illness, and the fight was exhausting me. I was becoming more and more tired as I lay on my bed, instead of more rested.

When I thought of Charles, I felt a pain in my heart and cried myself to sleep. I felt cheated. Why did the person I had fallen in love with have to be a wizard? Why did he have to be this kind of man? Why couldn't he have been just an ordinary man? But I laughed as I heard the voice of Grandmother in my head. I would never fall in love with just an ordinary man, because such a man would not interest me. I knew, whether I wanted to admit it to myself or not, that I was not an ordinary woman, that I was probably never going to lead an ordinary life, however ordinary it might look on the outside. My affinity was for events and people of an unusual nature. I loved a sense of magic and mystery.

Every once in a while I would wake up with strange tuggings in my solar plexus and in the muscles of my legs — almost a cramping but not quite. I went back to sleep after these episodes.

Later that evening when the moon was high, there was a knock at my door. Grandmother and Anne entered wearing dresses of white linen. Over Grandmother's arm was a similar dress meant for me. They woke me gently, sponged off my face, arms and legs, and helped me to get up. By this time I was so weak, I was not completely sure where I was. For a moment I thought I was home, and I talked to Grandmother as if she were my own mother.

"Shh," Grandmother said to me. "Say nothing. Gather your power as you will."

They dressed me in a white linen gown that was beautiful and fitted as if it were made for me. I did not have the strength to ask where it had come from or why they were putting it on me.

"It is for ceremonial purposes," Grandmother said, winking at me. "You will be fine, child. Do not fear," she said. "We are here to help you."

I nodded my head and smiled as best I could. They helped me out of the chamber and into the larger room of the cottage. I was surprised to see the only movement was the fire burning in the hearth. No one was there. Then Grandmother and Anne led me into the kitchen toward a door that I had always assumed led to a pantry. They went to it and threw open a wooden lock, then the heavy, creaking oak door, revealing a passageway.

I blinked my eyes in the dim lantern light and saw that there was a spiral staircase leading down and down and out of sight. The stairway was wide enough for me and Anne, with her arm around my waist and my arm around her shoulders, to stumble down toward the bottom, step by step. Anne bore most of my weight down the stairs. The stairs were stone, and niches in the wall held candles burning. I kept shaking my head and blinking, wondering if I were dreaming. I could not imagine that this stairway had been under the cottage all this time and I had not known about it.

As we spiraled down we would stop every four steps or so, and Anne would say something in a language that I could not quite catch. Maybe it was Gaelic. She would light a candle and ring a bell, and we would move a little further down, and then she would repeat the ritual—as if we were moving in stages downward. She made no explanation to me.

Finally, we reached the bottom of the stairway and found ourselves in a vast cavern under the earth. As I looked into the shadows, I saw the faces of many people, and I realized that they were standing or sitting in a circle around a design that had been drawn on the cavern floor. It was a cross, many circles, one on top of the other, and symbols that I did not recognize. I recognized no one in the room and in the dark could make out only part of their faces. They were also obscured by hanging cloth veils, behind which they stood or sat. I kept blinking my eyes, thinking I must truly be dreaming. I wondered what the gauzelike veils were used for. Toward the back I could see the shadow of someone standing at a large, flat stone that looked like a table.

Anne and Grandmother led me up to the first veil. It was like a long curtain hung across the cavern accenting an extraordinary design that

shone gold and silver in the floor. The design looked as if it were fashioned out of precious metals. I could identify at least three — bronze, silver, and gold. Anne sat me in a chair in front of the veils. I looked up at
the ceiling. It was ornate with designs of power and rune figures of all
sorts: stars, the galaxies. I felt as if I were sitting out in the countryside
looking up at a starlit sky. The Pleiades dominated one end of the cavern
ceiling.

Grandmother sat next to me, and Anne went to sit with the rest of the
people. I could barely keep myself upright in the chair. I was swaying
backward and forward. Grandmother held my arm.

"You must listen to me. There is an initiation into a higher level of
awareness about to happen." she said. "The veils in front of you represent
the levels of consciousness that we must proceed through in a lifetime. It
is important for you to see that you have lifted away the veils already as a
young girl."

"How did I do that, Grandmother?" I whispered.

"You became aware. That is first. You also began to become aware of
other realities besides the one in which you live."

"I did?" I asked.

"Yes, you did. You recognized Charles, and that is important."

"But I thought I had made a mistake," I said.

"It was no mistake, my child — it was a test."

For a moment I was angry. My eyes flashed at her, until I realized I did
not even have the energy to be angry now. "What am I supposed to do,
Grandmother?"

"We will help heal you, my child. First we had to see that you could
see."

After a moment, I nodded my head. "I understand."

I looked through the gauze veils and thought I saw whoever was standing on the other side of them move. And as I began to stare through the
veils, the first two parted as if by magic. The flat stone was actually placed
between the second and third veils and was as long as I was tall. It was low
and set with candelabras at either end. As Grandmother helped me to get
up and walked me to the stone, I noticed bowls of water, one brass and
one pewter, at either end, and bundles that were wrapped figures of Danu,
gold and silver symbols, runes, and herbs sprinkled around on the stone.

"Anne is a virgin," Grandmother said. "She gathered the water from a
running stream. It is an offering to the Goddess Mother and to the sun,
the father, to the moon who reflects our shining spirit, to Mother Earth,
who gives us life. This stone is the altar of Mother Earth. It is called a
sleeping stone, because it helps you to dream. You are an offering to

Mother Earth. Lie down on this altar now, Catherine, so that we can work with you to bring back your spirit."

Grandmother helped me to lie down. I noticed that my head was resting in the north.

"The people in this room are one with us," she said, putting one hand on my forehead and with the other, holding my hand. "They are here to lend us power, to hold a sacred spirit circle for us to work within. They are here to protect you and to guide you. Never fear. You are in a sacred place where you are protected from all harm."

I heard music from some corner of the cavern. It sounded like a stringed instrument and perhaps a harp and a flute. As it began to fill the air with celestial sounds, I swooned and moved in and out of sleep. Once, as I blinked my eyes I looked up and saw Charles standing over me. He was wearing a necklace with a talisman on the end, a circle with a cross, a diamond in the center, and four crosses within it for the four directions. It sparkled and shone in the candlelight, and somehow it seemed familiar to me. I shook my head trying to clear away the cobwebs in my mind. Charles just smiled broadly and told me that he was happy to see me.

"I know where your spirit shield is," he whispered in my ear, "for mine has been in the same place. I know the road. I will find her for you and bring her back."

Then placing his hand underneath my head, he helped me to lean forward just enough to sip from a pewter cup a pungent, hot liquid that tasted like hot flower water, with a little bitterness to it.

He said, "Drink just a little. You will not need much."

Moments later—or what seemed moments later—the cavern filled with light, and the music became very much louder as if the musicians were standing close around me. I could hear choruses of angels, or perhaps the voices of the people sitting around me. The beauty of the music transported me; I felt free from my body, as if I could fly. It felt as if I were in the astral plane, but I knew that I was still in my body. I could not imagine what was happening, nor did I care. I simply lay there enjoying the play of colors on the gilt ceiling of the cavern.

"Roll your eyes up." I heard Charles's voice in my ears. "Stare at the ceiling. Stare at the cross in gold above you."

As I stared at the cross above me, I realized that it was not the ceiling. It was in the necklace that Charles was wearing. He was holding it above me. I stared at the mirrorlike diamond in the center of the cross, and I could see the reflection of my own eye inside it.

"Keep looking into the eye. It is your own eye. Stare into the pupil of your eye," Charles said.

As I did that, I began to feel as if the eye were getting closer and closer, as if my own being were merging with the eye and becoming the eye, as if it were no longer my eye, but the eye of the cross itself. Then I felt a surge of energy or some kind of spurt or knock on the back of my neck. I heard a grinding or cracking sound like a log being split apart.

"Let your consciousness move into the eye," Charles said in my ear as he touched my forehead between my eyes with his finger.

Suddenly I moved into the eye and found myself out on the other side. I was in a field, a green field. It was a beautiful summer day, and I was looking at a sacred hill that loomed high out of the flat field. It looked like the sacred tor in Glastonbury, but it was not. Off in the distance I saw Charles waving to me, beckoning me to come toward him. I was wearing my white dress. I could not wait to be near him, so I ran across the field. As I reached him, he grabbed my hand, leaned down, and kissed me. Then, hand in hand, he led me toward what looked like earth mounds at the foot of the tor.

I realized that it was a maze. "This is the maze of the sleeping stone," Charles said. "It is covered in such a way that it looks like a series of labyrinthine mounds. In fact, it is a labyrinth for your initiation into power." He led me to the door, and he opened the door. He turned around and he said, "Are you ready?"

I nodded my head. "Yes." Somewhere my consciousness did not seem so sure, but it did not matter, because another part of me, the instinctual part of me, knew I could manage whatever happened. I was surprised at my own courage.

"Tell me what I must do," I urged Charles, in perfect faith that he would not mislead me.

"Catherine, I know that you have the power to move through this labyrinth and find your way out. When I close this door, it will be up to you. You must use the power around your navel. The power of Wyrrd will lead you—if you let it. I do not doubt that you know how to follow your will."

"What am I looking for?" I asked him.

"You are looking for your own spirit shield. Only you can retrieve what has been lost. You gave away your spirit, and you must bring her back. I can help you, but I cannot do it for you."

I placed my hands on the stones that marked the archway, the entrance to the labyrinth and realized what the earth was asking of me, the power it was going to take to find my way through. I knew I would die if I failed, and that I had only a short time to find my way. The stones felt cold under my palms, but worn. They had been touched for centuries by other hands. I wondered what had led other people to stand at this awesome threshold.

I looked down into the tunnel in front of me. I saw only darkness, but I was not afraid. My state of mind was quite unlike that of ordinary waking life. I seemed to be in a warrioress place of power within myself, undaunted and unshakable in my love for Charles. He reached out to take my hand and looked directly into my eyes for a long moment.

"You are a great warrioress," he said, as if he had been reading my mind. "I want you to be my partner, not only in this life, but in many lives to come. We have worked together before, and we will work together again. I want you to live, and I want you to live by my side, not as a mortal wife, but as a spirit wife and a partner. We can avail ourselves of each other's power and support. It is all that we can ask of each other at this time. Do you understand what all this means?"

I nodded my head, for somewhere inside me I did seem to know.

"I do understand, Charles. I love you, and now a part of me no longer wants you as a husband in the physical life. To confine us in our spirits to the life, the mundane life, of man and wife seems unfitting for the proud, extraordinary character of our love. I know that you feel it, that it is living as a child between us. And yes, I will work with you until I die."

I turned and took the candle that he handed me already lit.

"The candle will only burn for a short time. After I close the door you must walk down the labyrinth and find your way to the top."

"What do you mean 'the top'?"

"These are the only hints I can give you," Charles said. "You will feel as if you are moving upward, and you will come to a place where you can go no further. At that point there will be a stone over your head. You must raise your power with everything that is in you, and move the stone, and come back to me. That is the test. Good-bye, my love, for now." And he closed the door.

Instead of being frightened I was filled with excitement at the gravity of this test. It was life or death. I knew that he could not come in here after me if I lost my way. I gripped the candle holder and watched the tiny flame as it began to sputter and burn down. I walked as quickly as I could down the darkening tunnel. It was just wide enough for me to walk and tall enough for a man to stand upright.

The candle burned out. I blinked my eyes, trying to accustom them to the pitch blackness. But I could see absolutely nothing. Ordinarily, the closeness of the space would have made me scream. But instead I listened. There was no sound. I reveled in the silence. The feeling and smell of middle earth was all around me. It felt good. I listened some more, taking a deep breath. And then I heard a strange little voice way off in the distance. It said, "Follow me," in a whisper. It sounded like an old woman, and I thought, "Could it be the elves of middle earth have come to save me?" At just that moment, I heard what I thought was a little rasping giggle.

I had been friends with the elves all my life; they have rescued me from one scrape or another. I remembered once as a little girl, I had cornered a badger quite by accident when I was on my horse. My horse became very frightened and was rearing and whinnying in terror. The elves had come and placated the badger then led my horse away. They had been my friends. I had never known exactly why, but they had always watched over me, and I knew they were here now. And I knew it was all right to have whatever allies I could muster. How I got out of the labyrinth did not matter, as long as I could get out of there and find my spirit.

I thought I saw a flicker of light, a reflection of something red up ahead.

"Cross your eyes," I heard the little voice say. "Carefully," I heard. "Walk silently, using your power center as Grandmother has taught you. This is a test. Use every ounce of will and truth that is within you. Perceive and follow the sounds ahead of you."

I walked slowly, my arms stretched out in front of me, terrified at first that I was going to fall off a ledge or run into something. And then I lowered my arms and started walking more quickly. I realized that I had very little time. I had not the luxury of fear. I must hold myself together with all the strength I had. So I followed the little sounds, and I realized it must be flint that I was hearing. They were striking flint (or something was striking flint) along the cave walls. I would see a little flash of flint and hear a little sound, so subtle I was not sure whether I was imagining it. I did not care. It seemed to be working; I was not running into anything.

Finally I came to a Y-shaped intersection in the tunnel, and I did not know whether to go to the right or to the left. Then I heard a little sound — "Down to the left" — and I went that way. I got to a certain point, and I realized we were walking around a curve. We came to another split in the tunnel. Again, I saw a little strike of flint, a spark in the air. This time the underground passage went off to the right.

What seemed like hours passed, and I was getting so extraordinarily tired I could hardly move my legs. Somehow I knew that this journey through the labyrinth, like many spiritual tasks, was meant to strengthen my will and my courage and force me to grow. I needed to grow to regain my spirit. I needed to find my way through the darkness and trust that the Old One would mirror my efforts at the end.

I forced myself on, somehow able to take one more step, and one more. Finally, I felt the ground beneath my feet begin to rise, and I walked toward the end of the tunnel. I could still see absolutely nothing. I reached up to feel above me. The tunnel narrowed, and the ceiling got lower. I placed my arms against the slab of cold stone that formed the top of the tunnel, and with all my might I began to push, wondering how, exhausted as I was, I could ever lift this slab out of my way.

I saw several little sparks of light and heard a grinding sound and then a crack like the one I had heard when I had sipped the flower water that Charles had given me — the sound like a tree branch breaking away from its trunk. And then the great stone began to move. With a final thrust, with strength I did not even know I possessed, I gave the stone a great shove, and it moved out of the way and rolled back away from the opening. Brilliant moonlight shone down on my head and into the tunnel. As I blinked and looked up toward the moon, I realized I was at the bottom of the tor, and at its top, I saw the silhouette of a woman standing in a white linen dress with her arms extended toward the sky. And in the brilliant bars of moonlight spreading over the valley and the fells, I saw an enormous peregrine falcon, shrieking his hunting cry as he circled above us and dove down with a flap of billowing wings etched in silvery light from the moon. He swooped down and landed on the woman's arm. I thought this must be the mystery woman I had seen before.

As I climbed out of the tunnel, I felt an urge to run up the tor toward the woman, who was standing with her back toward me. As I ran closer to her, she slowly turned around. She held a shield in her right hand covered with stars. Suddenly I was looking at myself. Our eyes met, and I must have fainted, for that was the last thing I remembered.

I awoke on the sleeping stone in the cavern below Grandmother's house. The veils had been torn away, and Grandmother was standing over me rubbing my hands and helping me to sit up.

"It is good, my child. You have been healed. Your spirit shield has been restored to you."

CHAPTER · 20

A
CIRCLE
OF
ENCHANTMENT

I AWOKE THE MORNING after the ceremony feeling re-vitalized. As I lifted myself out of bed, I realized that although my body felt bruised, actually it was my spirit that hurt. The pain was in the interior of my body. My spirit felt beaten up, as if it had somehow been reshaped, and I was still sore from the process. I gingerly let the thought of Charles come into my mind. To my relief, he no longer made me tremble with longing. Instead I felt a warmth and a closeness to him. I explored the feeling as I lay back on my pillows. I knew a depth of love that I had experienced only with Grandmother. This was different; it was a woman's love for a man. But it was not a sexual love; it was a kinship of spirit. I knew that deep in my soul, deep in my heart, we understood each other, we had a place together in the universe. We were twin stars shining together in the heavens; our light commingled, but we were separated by an indeterminate amount of space. Somehow that was all right now. I was amazed that last night's ceremony could have changed me so totally. I had truly thought I would die of my love for him. Now all that seemed silly and stupid. I had learned something.

I leapt up from the bed, threw on my clothes after splashing some water on my face from the basin, combed my hair quickly and tied it back, and ran out to find Grandmother. I looked around at her cottage. Everything was normal. Nothing had changed. Alice was gone, and Grandmother was setting out eggs and bread and butter and honey for us. She motioned for me to sit next to her, patting the table with the palm of her hand, her topaz ring picking up the sunlight streaming through the window and reflecting it in the golden prism of color. I quickly sat down next to her and smiled brightly at the old woman, who was smiling back at me. She shook her head.

"It is good to see your spirit shining through your eyes again, Catherine. I have missed that light." She pinched my cheek and lifted up her cup for a long sip.

"Did all that really happen to me?" I asked. "I know that I went through a ceremony last night. I remember it, but it seems like a dream."

"All of life seems like a dream," Grandmother said with a wink.

"Grandmother, when I think of the rest of the world, when I think of the village, when I think of London, what it might be like to live at Court all the time, it feels as if they are a million miles away from me, as if this world is not as it seems. There is so much left for me to learn. No matter what I learn, I feel that I have learned nothing."

I licked some honey off my spoon. Grandmother gazed absently at me for a long time as if her mind were very far away. At last she reached forward and picked up a glass vase that was sitting in the center of the table. As she held it up to the light, the sun reflected through it in rainbow-like colors.

"Look at this vase, my daughter. What do you see?" she asked.

"I see a clear vase, and I see that it is empty inside, and I see the light reflecting through it. It looks beautiful."

"How is this vase like time?" Grandmother asked.

I studied it for a long while, and finally, not knowing really what else to say, "It is empty."

"That's interesting, Catherine, because, in a sense, time is empty. In a way, time is outside of nothingness."

"I do not understand," I said, "but I sense what you mean."

"There is a space," she said, "between you and me. There is an emptiness between us. There is a space between you sitting there and your family back where you live. Is that right?" she asked.

"Yes," I said.

"And for you to cover that space, you would have to go from here to where they live, and it would take you time to get home. Is that right?"

"Yes," I said. "But I still do not understand what you mean."

"I mean that you can fill space with time, your idea of what time is. You can also fill space with other things. Is that right?"

"Yes, I guess so," I said.

"And sometimes space can be very small, and you can fill it with something larger than the space."

"Oh, Grandmother, now I really do not understand."

"Here, let me show you," the old woman said.

She lifted up the vase, and she said, "Now look through the vase. Look through the glass out the window to your horse grazing on the grass outside."

I stood up and looked through the vase, and I saw my horse grazing outside.

"All right. I see my horse through the glass."

"Very well," she said. "Now you have filled this vase with your horse. You see, you look outside and you see your horse standing inside your vase. That would be one way to describe it. Is that right?"

"Yes, I guess so."

"Is the vase smaller than your horse?"

"Yes," I said.

"Now do you see? You have filled the space inside that vase with something larger than the space inside the vase." Grandmother giggled, and so did I.

"You are right, Grandmother. I have done just that."

"You were asking me about Charles, how he can be as old as I am."

"Yes, that is right. I do not understand that. What could he possibly have meant?"

"In a way, Catherine, it means that he filled space with something larger than this space. It has to do with time. Have you ever thought much about time?"

"Yes, I have, Grandmother. I remember not long ago, when I went out of my body, time passed incredibly quickly. I was outside my body and only a few minutes had passed in my mind, and when I came back into my body, half the day was gone. Is that what you mean?"

"Yes, in part, Catherine. I am talking about the fact that maybe, as you have seen in the ceremony last night and in all our work together, life is not completely as it appears. You have to begin to stretch your imagination. Go to the limits of your consciousness and begin to work on different planes of existence so that we can move into other levels. What Charles wants to do with you and what I want to teach you is a way of filling space with something larger than you think could ever fit into that space. And you can do that through shifts in time. Perhaps Charles is much larger than you think he is. He can barely fit into the space of this lifetime, because his lifetimes together would never fit into the area that is allotted him in this lifetime. It is possible to be much older than you think you are. It is possible to live a very long time."

"Grandmother, do you mean that you have found the secret of eternal life? I have heard my mother talk about that. I have heard there are some people — alchemists, I think — who know such things. Is that what you are talking about?"

"Yes, my child, it is something like that." Grandmother giggled to herself and took another bite of her bread.

"Part of it has to do with distance," she went on to say. "Your horse outside is very tiny when you look through the vase; he fits inside it. If you were to move the vase closer to him, then the vase would be more likely to fit inside him."

I laughed at that analogy.

"When we move closer to things, they change. When we move farther away, their proportions become different. Time is like that. You can move in and out of time. Your life seems very big now because it is all you know. It may even be possible to become larger or smaller."

"Do you mean that if I were smaller, I would fit in different spaces than I do now?"

"Well, that is partially true. Of course, you would be taking up a different kind of space. But I am talking about a more important space. I am talking about space and time and how they relate to each other. I am talking about the secrets of life."

"But only God can create life."

"This is true, Catherine, but we are all God."

I was shocked that Grandmother would say that.

"But, Grandmother, what do you mean? Some people would call that blasphemy."

"Yes, some people would." Grandmother smiled. "But if you understand that God made us in his likeness, what else could that mean?"

I thought about her question for some time.

"I see what you are saying, Grandmother. If we are like God, then we can only be God. Is that what you mean?"

"Oh, I think it is more than that. A robin is like a hawk, but it is also different," Grandmother said. "The Goddess Mother created us as reflections of herself. God to me is the Great Mother. God to me is the Old One. But it does not really matter; God is God. Life force is life force, and it takes many forms. God is the creator, the Great Spirit that permeates all of us. Once you truly understand that, Catherine, you realize that we are all part of one another, that we are in agreement on this wonderful, green earth, and that we live in a state of duality, a state of separateness that is not real. We are separated by an agreement called space and time. You can move in and out of the dimensions of time."

Grandmother went over to the cupboard and picked out an onion and brought it back. She put it in front of me, and she began to carefully peel away the layers.

"We are peeling away the layers of time, as this onion peels away. We are beginning to understand in our work together, Catherine, that we need to get down to the core of existence. What is essential? If you were to peel away this onion, it would peel away into what?"

I thought for a moment about the many times I had watched our cook peel onions.

"There would be nothing there."

"That is right. There would be pure spirit," Grandmother said. "Maybe there are ways to move your essence around," she suggested.

"What do you mean, Grandmother?"

"Perhaps if you find the core of your existence, the Godness inside you, the Great Mother inside you, perhaps it would be nothing except the spirit, the essence. And when you find that essence, you can move that essence into any shape that you desire. You could be the horse inside that vase or the vase inside the horse. Or you yourself could move your essence into the interior of that vase, and if you could do that, you could do anything."

I shook my head as I thought about what Grandmother had said, wondering what she was really getting at.

"I think I am missing something, Grandmother. I am not sure what you are trying to tell me."

"Do you feel confused, with many different images in your mind?" Grandmother asked.

"Yes," I said.

"Good," she said. "That is just what I want you to feel. I want you to think about this. You see, Charles understands much of what I am talking to you about."

"Grandmother, can you explain to me why Charles needs to be alone in this lifetime? I understand what he said, that he is a wizard and he needs his full energy. But is there anything more you can tell me?"

"Let me try to explain it in a different way. When I ask you to sit with your back against the tree and meditate, what happens after you do that for several hours? Tell me how it is you feel."

"Well, I feel a settling inside me. A quietness that comes over me, and finally I get to a point where I feel a oneness with myself, where I feel as if there is no one in the universe that I need. I move into a state of bliss that is very difficult for me to describe, really."

"But you do not need to say anything more, Catherine. It is that state of bliss that I want you to think about. And I think you have hit on exactly what I am talking about. You said that you feel as though you need no one else. Is that correct?"

"Yes, Grandmother, that is the way I feel."

"But ordinarily you feel you do need someone. Is that correct?" Grandmother asked.

"Yes, that is true, Grandmother. When I am not in that state of oneness, I feel quite different. I feel the need for company, for someone to share my life with. When I move into that state of bliss, I need no one. I want no one."

"It is that state of bliss, Catherine, that Charles is living in now. He has been able to perfect himself in the power of Wyrrd to the point where he needs no one. For him taking a wife would be to lose that state of bliss."

We both laughed at the image that her words created. And then Grandmother became very serious again.

"It is important that you understand this about Charles, because you have yourself experienced for a moment the way he lives all the time. You have experienced a little bit of how you will be able to live, in a profound way, when you are older."

"How do you mean, Grandmother? I am not sure I understand you."

"Charles has perfected his art to such a high degree that he needs only himself, and his God, the power of Wyrrd. In a sense he lives all the time in a quality or state of love that most people find only in the act of love. One day you will speak with Charles about this," Grandmother said, "because he can explain it in a way that perhaps will be more meaningful to you."

"I think I understand. Thank you, it makes sense to me now. But what I would also like to know, Grandmother, is why you never told me that you were the beautiful woman down on the jetty. You were the Lady of the Mist, yet you never mentioned it to me. Why?"

Grandmother smiled rather sheepishly. "I think we have been talking enough, my daughter. It is time we went to work in the garden; there is a lot to do. And later we will need to go into the forest to find herbs."

"But, Grandmother, that is not fair. You really must tell me how this has all happened. It was such a shock to me. At first I was very angry."

"I understand, Catherine, why you were angry. You felt deceived. But if I had told you earlier, would you even have believed me?"

I thought for some time, but finally I had to shake my head.

"No, Grandmother, you are right. I probably would not have believed you."

"There, you see?" Grandmother said. "Let us go to work."

She gathered her shawl and her velvet bag that she always used to collect her roots and herbs, I gathered mine, and we went outside. The garden was bathed in sunlight and smelled of rich earth and honeysuckle. I took a deep breath. It was good to feel so relaxed and at peace, and I decided I had been healed completely. It was wonderful to have respite from my emotions, and I lost myself in the gardening with Grandmother.

CHAPTER 21

SACRED DREAM

Songs patterned after religious fervor
songs patterned after the mind of waste
songs patterned after the dream of rhythms
where the word and world enters
in
and then magic begins.
Here
is where
to light the
top of the ladies fair and wondrous
candle
or burden
who's to say?
And falling
would be no easier than reluctance
and the slips
of nature
make the snow dissolve
soon in crystal-laden England
and Beauty Lake is real,
is named,
is forgotten.

THE NEXT DAY I SPENT riding my horse down to Collingham's lake, where I had first seen Grandmother, or the Lady of the Mist, standing on the jetty, the beautiful woman with the cape made of fog. I had a sense of carefree abandon, as if I did not have a worry in the world. We galloped over the hills, jumped over dry stone walls, and splashed through Brixworth's river. My horse seemed happy to have my full attention once again. As he galloped, I would lean forward on his neck. His silken mane felt like wheat blowing in the wind against my face. I felt as if I had been through an initiation. I had left childhood behind and moved into a new period of my life. My feelings for Grandmother, Alice, Anne, and Charles had deepened even more — if such a thing were possible. But not only had my feelings widened and become more mature, they had taken on a quality of order. For the first time in my life I truly knew why I was alive. I did not know the end result of all of this work with Grandmother, but I did know that I felt the Goddess Mother, the Old One, deep inside me. I felt the strength and purity of Danu's power, and I felt a oneness with her. For the first time I felt deserving of the attention she had so obviously given me. The prospect of learning more was exciting. I knew that I had barely touched the edge of a great island of magic. Perhaps I had walked on the shore a little. But I knew now that I was beginning a long climb into the interior of that island. I was frightened and thrilled and excited by the adventure.

I stopped and dismounted by the shore of Collingham's lake, where I sat and meditated for a long time, gazing into the waters and breathing in the scent of damp earth and grasses. By the time I got up and led my horse along the shore, a mist had gathered over the water. A wind from the south lifted the mist and swirled it around me. My horse snorted and reared back against the reins.

"It's all right, boy," I said as I patted his neck and calmed him down. "Easy, easy," I said as I led him on through the mist. It was now swirling around our feet and enveloping our heads and moving even higher in a funnel.

I could see nothing in front of me. I had never seen fog so dense, and fog that collected in this way so suddenly. I heard water lapping against the sand off to my left, otherwise I would not have even known where the lake was. I was not really frightened, but I was amazed. If we moved to the right, away from the lake, I reasoned, certainly the fog would disperse. We picked our way up the sandy beach, me in the lead, my horse, still nervous, following. All of a sudden a strong wind came up swirling the fog in a dervish dance around us. I could not see to move in any direction, so finally I sat down right in front of my horse, stroking his legs to keep him calm. "Perhaps I should just wait this out," I thought to myself. "If the wind is blowing this strongly, the fog will have to blow over. There was not a cloud in the sky before the fog crept in." My horse was so nervous and jerking the reins so hard that I decided to tie him to the tree right beside us, in case he was to jerk unexpectedly and pull free from my grip.

It was then that I thought I heard the sound of a flute playing ever so gently, ever so softly. I strained my ears, wondering where the music could be coming from. Then it was gone. I thought it must have been my imagination. Then it came again, this time closer.

"Catherine, over here," I heard a voice say. It was a man's voice. I turned to the left, straining my eyes to see through the fog, still thick and swirling around us. A silvery golden light pierced the fog as if the sun were shining down. And out of the light I started to see a form emerging. I stared hard at it, becoming more and more frightened. Suddenly the figure came close, and I recognized Charles.

"Catherine, come this way. Follow me."

"I cannot leave my horse," I said.

"Do not worry, Catherine. We will be close by. The fog will only last a short time."

My horse did seem quite calm, which surprised me. I turned and took Charles's hand. He walked me just a yard or two away and sat me down on a blanket that he had spread on the sand. The air around it was quite warm, almost like summertime.

"Where have you come from?" I asked Charles, bewildered at seeing him.

"It does not matter where I have come from. It only matters that I am here, and that you can see me."

I was puzzled at his choice of words. "Of course, I can see you," I said.

"I am not really here," he said to me, smiling at my look of bafflement.

"Well, if you are not really here, then my name is not Catherine, because I certainly can see you."

"Yes, I understand, but you are only seeing my power. You are not really seeing me."

I looked at him for a long moment, not knowing exactly what he meant, but then I remembered what Grandmother had told me; Charles was a wizard, and he could be in two places at the same time.

"Do you mean—"

As if he had sensed my thoughts, Charles nodded his head. "Yes, and I have something I want to talk to you about," he said. "First I need to know how you are feeling after our ceremony."

I told him everything, that I was feeling relieved and healed and quite at ease, that I felt as if I had been through an initiation.

"Yes, Catherine, you have been through an initiation without even knowing it. You have passed well, and I am proud of you. Now I would like to teach you more about oneness and the kind of freedom I need to remain a wizard in this lifetime."

"What do you mean?" I asked.

"I can only show you," he said. "You must trust me. You must trust that what I am about to show you is something sacred. I want to show you how to make love, but in a way that brings our spirits together as one."

My eyes widened. "What do you mean, Charles? You want to make love?" The fog was forming gray plumes above us.

"Yes, that is what I said."

"But I thought you told me you could not take a wife. I could not make love to anyone before I take a husband. It would not be fitting."

"You are always a virgin to me, and when we have made love, you will still be a virgin. I want to make love to you in spirit. I want to show you one of the highest arts of magic, and perhaps then you can understand why I must always be alone. Whether to always be alone yourself will then be your choice. It is up to you, but I want you to know about the alternatives. Most people never have that choice."

He looked at me and I could feel him stroking my hair. My luminous fibers began to loosen and my spirit shield to fringe out past my physical form. We were completely surrounded in fog, as if we were covered by a veil. I felt as if he were caressing me, as if he were kissing my neck and my breasts. It was the first time that any man had ever touched me thus. He was wonderfully gentle and I felt great love for him. I lost myself in my first sexual experience. It was as if I no longer existed and he no longer existed. It was as if we were one, completely merged in body and being. There was no world; there was no fog; and there was no earth. I cared about nothing but beingness. In his arms, with our energy intermixed, feeling the surge of the universe around us, I felt as if we had turned into pure energy and pure light.

When finally the light subsided and I came back into separateness, back into feeling alone, he carefully dressed me, caressing me lovingly and with respect. I would never forget my first loving. I would never forget Charles.

Then he sat across from me, took both my hands, and said, "Tell me how you felt when we made love."

I was very shy, and I laughed nervously at first. Then finally I was able to tell him about the extraordinary oneness I had felt. I admitted I had forgotten my body and his and felt part of the stars, of the universe, of nothingness.

He said, "That is it!"

"What do you mean?" I asked, surprised.

"That is it," he said. "Is it not akin to meditation? When you sit in meditation, when you do the practice that Grandmother has shown you, is it not something like that?"

I thought for a moment and nodded my head. "Yes, Charles, it is. I felt bliss. I felt a oneness with all life, a kinship. It is true."

"Grandmother, I know, has spoken to you about all this. Can you imagine, Catherine, having that orgasmic feeling throughout a great part of your life, not just for a moment?"

"No, I cannot imagine it. Is that even possible?" I asked.

"Yes, it is, and that is how I live my life. If you were to feel such a feeling for days on end, Catherine, would you want to give it up for an earthly love, give it up to be married, to have children? Would you even consider it?"

I thought about what he was saying. "No, I would not, Charles. I would never want to give it up, it would be too extraordinary to even think of giving up. I cannot imagine how wonderful it would be if I had that kind of energy and that possibility within my being. Think of the healing I could do." Then I realized something else. "Think of the healing you can do, Charles. Perhaps you could heal all of England. Perhaps with your power, you can reinstate the Goddess, the Great Mother, to her rightful position in life. Maybe you can help people to understand how to live in harmony instead of fighting and living in pain and fear."

"Perhaps, Catherine, you really understand. I hope you truly understand this was not a trick. I felt that I must come to you and share this gift with you so that you would understand that it is something that you can find in your life. You can attain what I have attained. Anyone can. It is a matter of training and dedication and purity of spirit. I will help you to find that place within your own soul. Our spirits will never meet again like this in this lifetime. But you needed to know, so that when someone does ask you to marry him, someone who can be a man for you, a husband, you can make the choice. If you take an earthly husband, you cannot reach the heights, because you will need to use your energy and attention for earthly endeavors. You can still do great things with your learning, however. Perhaps this is not your path. It is only for you to know."

I stood up with Charles and hugged him. Then he turned me around and took me back to the tree. My horse was grazing underneath it on a little patch of grass and seemed perfectly fine. I turned to say good-bye to Charles, but he was gone. I smiled to myself. I had never felt so complete. I was so grateful to him—I hoped I had remembered to thank him. As I stood thinking about Charles, the fog began to dissipate. The wind died down. The mist settled down again over the lake and began to curl off into the rushes and the reeds on the opposite shore, finally disappearing altogether. I shook my head, wondering if I had been dreaming. As I got back on my horse and rode at a brisk trot toward home, I laughed to myself in wonder at the way I was thinking that everything happening to me seemed to be out of a dream. I knew that I had not lost my virginity to Charles, but I had lost my virginity of spirit. Physically, I was unchanged, but in my soul, I was changed forever. How could one ever be the same after making love to a wizard, a Prince of Light?

CHAPTER·22

THE
SISTERS
OF
WYRRD

Here is a fine
degree of clarity
that burrows
into the palm
of the hand
with energy
voiceless
imaginary
more real than lightning of mind.

I AWOKE IN THE Dreamlodge with Agnes and Ruby sitting anxiously near me. They helped me remove my necklace and placed it back on my altar. They smudged me with sage and made me walk around for an hour or so and then let me go back to the cabin and sleep. When I awoke to eat dinner, I felt fairly rested. The memories of my dreaming clamored inside my head, wanting to be shared. But Agnes and Ruby seemed very remote.

After eating dinner with them in unusual silence, I finally sat back in my chair and said, "Okay, Agnes and Ruby, both of you are acting very strangely. Why are you looking at me that way?" The bundles of drying herbs, drums, rattles, and feathers that hung from the rafters threw strange curved designs on the shadowed walls.

Agnes and Ruby glanced at each other and sat back shaking their heads. They looked like a couple of old crones as they started to elbow each other, still looking at me in a very strange way.

"We're looking at you strangely," Ruby said, "because you're close-up dead, that's all."

"Oh, thanks a lot. What do you mean, I'm close-up dead?" I asked, suddenly frightened by the fact that they would even kid about something like being nearly dead.

Agnes reached across the table and placed her leathery palms over the back of my hand. "Your aura is very depleted, Lynn. That's why we are concerned."

"What do you mean, depleted?" I asked in alarm.

"You have done a lot of work on the other levels of consciousness, and your physical self is telling the tale."

"I still don't understand," I said, taking a deep breath of pine-scented air.

"You're tired," Ruby said, clucking her tongue.

I thought for several minutes about what they were saying, and finally I nodded in agreement. "Yes, I am tired. In fact, I'm absolutely exhausted. But it's a funny thing. I really don't feel physically tired. I'm suffering from a kind of nervous exhaustion; there's a buzzing going on inside me, and yes, my physical self is really quite centered and fine," I said.

Ruby came over to stand behind me. She began pressing her thumbs into the back of my neck. Agnes closed her eyes almost entirely, so that little glints of silver and light were showing from beneath lids that were not quite closed.

"Look at me," she ordered. "Look into my eyes."

I looked into her eyes and found it very difficult to concentrate, particularly with Ruby poking the back of my neck till it hurt. I knew better than to ask her what she was doing to me.

"Now take a deep breath," Agnes said, "and begin to watch your breathing. Concentrate on your breath going in and out."

I did this for several minutes and began to relax.

"Now close your eyes," Agnes said, "and listen to the voices in your head."

I closed my eyes, and immediately the buzzing inside my body became more intense. As if Agnes could tell what was happening, she asked me, "Little Wolf, the buzzing inside you—does it remind you of anything?"

For several minutes I listened to the buzzing, unable to place where I had heard that noise before. It was very different from the usual white sound I heard when I was working with energy centers inside my body. I searched my memory, unable to remember. As the buzzing became louder and yet more irregular, it suddenly dawned on me.

"Agnes, it sounds like the buzzing of bees."

Ruby poked me even harder on the back of my neck. "Listen more carefully. Be more aware," Ruby commanded.

"Take another deep breath," Agnes said. "Go even deeper into your power center and listen carefully and remember," she ordered.

I breathed deeply and was aware of my spirit shield wanting to leave my body.

"Don't let your spirit shield leave your body," Ruby ordered, as if she too were sensing my feeling of transition.

I nodded my head and continued to concentrate on my breathing. As I listened more deeply and more carefully to the buzzing sound, I realized that the buzzing was actually a very fast flapping of wings, like those of a hummingbird, only thousands of wings. And then I realized what it was. It was the sisters of Wyrrd. There was no question. My eyes opened in astonishment. I stared at Agnes, and Agnes realized that I knew what I was hearing.

"It's the sisters of Wyrrd, isn't it?" I said, feeling very shaky, as though I had a foot in two worlds. For a moment I felt I was being torn in half. "How could I hear the sisters of Wyrrd when I'm not in that time?" I asked, looking back and forth at both of them with terror written all over me.

Ruby stopped poking me in the back of my neck, and as she stopped, the flapping of the wings became more distant, more like a humming sound. She began to stroke the back of my neck and rub my shoulders with her strong fingers. It felt good, and I began to relax. Agnes came over to me and looked very closely into my eyes, as if she were an eye doctor, reading the imprints in my irises.

"You are hearing the sounds of another time. It is a great mystery," Agnes said.

"Humph," Ruby said. "It's no mystery at all. You are exhausted and your being is fringing off into another time, because your spirit shield is simply too tired to carry the weight of two worlds. I believe your teacher, your grandmother, spoke to you about placing something larger in a very small space?"

I spun around to look at Ruby. "How could you possibly know that? I haven't told you about that yet."

"Well, just say that it's part of my very special abilities," Ruby said, cocking her head to one side and putting her hands on her hips.

"I must say, that's very impressive, Ruby," I said in awe, not wanting her to know how absolutely amazed I really was. I looked at her again and repeated what I had said before. "How could you have possibly known that, Ruby? Truly, I want to know. It's frightening to me that you can so completely read everything that goes through my mind."

"Oh, it's nothing. Don't worry. I won't infringe on your privacy, Lynn."

Agnes interrupted, "Little Wolf, when you journey as far away as you have, do you think for one minute that we would let you go unattended and unguarded? Do you realize how much harm could have been done to you if we hadn't been there standing as your guardians?"

Tears came to my eyes as I looked across at Agnes, who was now standing on the other side of the table sipping some tea. For several minutes I said nothing.

"Thank you," I finally said, turning to each of them and giving each a hug. "I really am so extraordinarily naive," I said. "Thank you for taking care of me."

As we sat back down around the table together, Agnes looked across at me. "It is time, Lynn, to bring an end to your journey with Grandmother."

I looked at her, knowing that she was right, yet feeling hollow inside. Tears came to my eyes, as I thought of how terribly alone I would feel without Grandmother; we had bonded so profoundly.

"I don't know how I will manage without her. Oh, Agnes, how can I bear the grief of separation? I'm finding myself very ragged and frightened."

"Well, that's certainly nothing new," Ruby said, tapping her finger hard like a stick on the table.

I raised my eyebrows at Ruby and said nothing, knowing that actually she was very right. I just didn't want to admit it. "Does this mean that I can never journey back to see her?" I asked, afraid to hear their answer.

Agnes thought for a long while. Finally, she tilted her head from side to side, the candlelight reflecting off her high cheekbones giving her face an angular quality.

"Your work with Grandmother is not yet finished. In fact, you are just beginning to know her, but I don't believe that you are strong enough to continue this work right now. So your journey must finish at this point. Perhaps at another time you will be able to go back into that lifetime and work with Charles and work with Grandmother and learn the rest of the mysteries that you so desperately need to know about. But your spirit shield is weakened to the point that the work is very dangerous for you. I want you to go back one more time. We will help you keep your shield strong, but we can only do that one more time. It will be too dangerous for you to do it again anytime soon. Perhaps you will be able to remember something of this life as Catherine. Perhaps not, but Grandmother will help you and be able to communicate with you in some way. She is aware of everything. There is nothing that Grandmother does not know, so trust her — as we do — to do what is best for you."

"Do you mean to say, Agnes, that Grandmother is in communication with you in some way?"

After several minutes and several sips of tea, Agnes looked up at me with great kindness.

"The Sisterhood is a circle. It is a circle that lives beyond the limits of time and space. Whether we are incarnate in the physical form or whether we have chosen our death in the physical dimension and have gone on to work in other dimensions, the circle is always the circle. We will never lose each other again. You are young, and you are young to this work. Even though you have been doing the work of the Great Mother for many lifetimes, you are still young compared with the rest of us.

"There are many things that you still do not know, but as you are able to travel the dimensions of the universe, as you are able to avail yourself of the energy of the stars and mother earth and the harmony of all that lives, you will begin to see that all of life is a circle, that all beings that are alive are part of that circle, that in fact, though we become lost in the dream of duality, the dream of separateness, we are in fact all reflections of the Great Spirit. We are all indeed part of the same spirit and the same God. We are indeed all one. We cannot lose each other on any level, but sometimes in our ignorance we forget the meaning of life, and we forget our destiny. What we do together is a process of remembering, of re-membering who we truly are.

"I am a mirror for you, as is Ruby, and as is Grandmother. We are mirrors for different parts of you that need to grow. Those mirrors will be there for you as long as you need them, and then when you need them one day no longer, we merge together like pieces of a puzzle finding their place interlocked with one another. It is all truth, and it is all light. We are that. Lie back into the arms of the Great Mother, and let her guide your path.

"Your shaman will has brought you to this point of power. It is time now to let your will rest. We are the stars in one another's universe forever."

Agnes got up from the table, as we all did, heading for bed and a very deep sleep.

The next morning we got up, said prayers to the rising sun, and ate a very simple breakfast. Agnes and Ruby accompanied me to the Dream-lodge. This was to be my last journey with Grandmother for perhaps a very long time. Part of me wanted to wait. I didn't want it to end. I took my amulet necklace off the altar and briefly held it to my heart before putting it on.

As I lay down on the sheepskins in the lodge, Agnes sat down beside me and held my hand.

"Do not allow your desire to keep Catherine and Grandmother alive in your life lessen your energy in this work. It is important to use the strength and power of your will to the utmost, because your spirit shield is very weak, and it needs every bit of power that you can muster. I am commanding you not to lose yourself in your emotions. It could be deadly for you. I know that you have the ability to sidestep your emotions if you absolutely have to, and this is one of those times. Do not lose your-self in your feelings, not now. There will be time for grieving, if you need it, when you come out of your trance, but now you must stay strong. Re-member who you are, Little Wolf. Do not waiver in your sacred dream."

Ruby had moved to my left side and tapped my chest with her finger to get my attention. She narrowed her eyes and squinted at me.

"Don't let the dream hook you," she said, hooking her finger in the side of her mouth like a perch on the end of a fishing line. I couldn't help but laugh at the hilarious distortion of her features; she really looked like a fish. Ruby never failed to lift me out of my obsession with the serious-ness of it all.

We all laughed as I closed my eyes and began to relax myself into my final dream journey. With my spirit shield so weak, it took me longer to quiet my energy and build it back up again so that I could move out of my body effectively and with the proper intent. At first I was aware of Agnes and Ruby sitting on either side of me. I was aware that they were doing something with their eagle fans, and then my awareness of the Dreamlodge and my two teachers faded away, and I found myself back in England. I remembered nothing of Agnes and Ruby and Lynn. My spirit shield was not strong enough to retain the imprint of other lifetimes. It was Grandmother in her wisdom who saved me.

CHAPTER · 23

THE
WOMAN
OF
WYRRD

IT WAS A BEAUTIFUL DAY. I sat out in the garden with Grandmother, looking at her roses and her other magnificent flowers blooming all around us.

"What is bothering you, Little One?" Grandmother asked me with a quizzical expression.

I looked at her sadly. "I do not know, Grandmother. I am just feeling very sad—and somehow apprehensive."

"What are you afraid of?"

"I do not know. It is an unnamed fear," I answered, "a foreboding that seems to be welling up inside my heart. I do not know how to explain it."

"Do you know what is needed when you feel this way?" Grandmother asked, taking a sip of her tea and inhaling the aroma of the flower petals that settled on the top of the water in her cup.

"No, Grandmother."

"Fear gives you a perfect opportunity to learn." She smiled at me with a twinkle in her eye. "It gives you the opportunity to witness, and when I say witness, I mean just to sit very silently and watch, not meditate, but just observe your feelings as they well up inside you, your feelings of pain, of whatever comes up. You need just to witness; watch what happens; do not make any movement or any judgment or choice. Just simply watch what happens."

"Why is that so important? Frankly, Grandmother, I do not know if I want to watch this, I feel so bad. I would like to look away and do something else."

"Ah, yes," Grandmother said. "That is what most people do. They try to make such feelings disappear by producing a desire—for you, a desire perhaps for Charles. Perhaps that was what was happening when you met Charles, at least part of it. You unconsciously created a desire in your life that would disguise the discomfort that you were feeling about being a woman of power in this lifetime, about being a special woman, something that you have great anxiety about. If you could fill that place inside you that feels anxiety with desire, you would no longer think about the pain."

I looked at Grandmother for a long time, thinking about what she had said, not knowing quite what to say. As I thought back about Charles and about my life in general, I realized that she was speaking the truth. In fact I had tried to cover up my anxiety with many desires.

"All you need do, Catherine, is simply witness. The witnessing will nourish the brilliance inside you. One day there will come a time when all your anxiety is gone. That is when your goddesshood will become most radiant. That is when you will become like the stars. We have talked

· 209 ·

much about returning to the stars. But you can never return to the stars until all anxiety is gone. If you begin to witness your anxieties instead of reacting to them, you will begin to realize that perhaps there is a pot of gold at the end of the rainbow. Perhaps, in fact, there is relief and there is true beauty in this human life of ours. Come, let us go talk to your horse for a few minutes."

"Why, Grandmother?"

"I want to show you something," she said, taking my hand and leading me out to the front of the cottage where my horse was tethered and grazing happily in the shade of a tree. He raised his head and whinnied as he saw us coming. We went over and patted him.

"This horse of yours, Catherine, is in a perfect state of being. This horse does not want to be anything other than what he is. He does not want to be a cat or a dog or a rosebush. He is just happy. He is in a perfect state of being. We, on the other hand, as human beings, are split. Part of us wants to be the goddess. Part of us wants to be the stars. And there is another part of us that just wants to be an animal, a creature that has no desires, that does not think, that has no anxiety, but we want that in a way that is not full of light and full of godliness, but just simply full of the instinctual nature. This horse is magnificent. And in a way, this horse is just like what you will become someday, except for one thing. Do you know what that is?" she asked me, her eyes squinting against the sunlight. I thought for a moment, then smiled at the old woman.

"Well, the difference is that we will be conscious that we have grown with our ability, that we have become free beings by becoming free from anxiety and free from the desires that tie us to the earthly plane."

Grandmother winked at me and pinched my cheek. "Yes, that is very close," she said. "Come. Let us go have some oatcakes."

She patted my horse, and he went back to his grazing. We walked back into the cottage, into the dimness, with the sunlight streaming through the higher windows leaving pools of yellow light on the stone floors.

Grandmother and I spent several hours that afternoon polishing silver and the brass bowls that she used in the ceremonies and drying herbs that she had gathered in the forest and the garden. We said very little. I still felt uneasy, as if something was about to happen. Finally, I could stand it no longer and I looked at Grandmother with a question in my eyes.

"Grandmother, is there something you are not telling me?"

The old woman reached into her apron pocket and brought out her Power Deck. This time she mixed the beautiful cards for several minutes with her eyes closed. Then she fanned them carefully in her left hand and held them out to me.

"Perhaps the power cards have something to tell us. Draw a card, Catherine."

The old woman's eyes sparkled sapphire blue in the shaft of sunlight coming through the window. I was almost afraid to read what the card had to say. It read:

> The first lesson of power is that we are alone.
> The last lesson of power is that we are all one.

I started to ask her a question, but Grandmother shushed me with a long finger over her lips. She knew that I understood. Very carefully, she gathered the cards and placed them in their intricately carved box and returned them to her pocket. She came over and touched my arm and said, "Come, Catherine, let us take a walk down to Brixworth's river."

Outside, as we walked into the garden, clouds gathered, the sunlight edging them in gold and purple light. A low fog had moved in from the lake and held close to the ground the way it does in the morning, as if the clouds had fallen to earth. Patches of green showed through the mist. Wrapping our shawls around head and shoulders, we walked down the path into the forest. The sunlight streamed down through the high trees in brilliant wands of light. We carefully lifted our skirts as we moved through the damp grass until we came to the slowly moving stream. We sat near Eywas Cross, whose ancient form threw a dark shadow at our feet. A brown sparrow sat on the tip of the stone cross, carrying a sprig of rosemary in its beak.

Grandmother seated herself on an old stump, and I sat next to her on a smooth stone partly covered with moss. The sound of the rippling water calmed me.

"Catherine, we have come to a time in life, really a time in your life, when you are standing at the forked trails."

I wondered what she meant. Answering my unasked question, she went on.

"Many choices will be made for you, my daughter. Your family will no doubt take you to London and to Court. I have spent many days while you were gone back home talking with the trees, and the language of the trees tells me that we may not be together for a while, at least not on this physical plane."

"But how can that be possible, Grandmother? I cannot live without you. I cannot leave you. I have asked my mother to let me stay at home."

Grandmother chuckled a little to herself, then reached out and held my hand. "Catherine, it would be wonderful if it were so, but I am afraid that you have many things to learn in this lifetime, and not all of these things will you learn with me. And that is good; that is the way it should be."

"But what about Charles? What about Alice and Anne? What am I going to do?"

"You will see Charles, and you will see Alice at Court. Anne and I will be here for you when you return. And perhaps — "

A glint of humor appeared on Grandmother's face. Her wrinkled skin seemed smooth for a moment, almost like a young girl's.

"I'm sure that we will see you in London as well. I have ways," she said.

I did not ask her what she meant; I knew that anything Grandmother wanted, she could manage to do.

"What do you mean, 'the language of the trees'?" I asked the old woman.

"The language of the trees is an ancient art that I learned a long time ago. We have not talked much about the sacredness of the trees and why the alder is a more sacred tree, perhaps, than a pine, although they are all sacred and they all have things to teach us. We will talk more about that one day, but let it be known now that the weeping willow is your friend. When the wind moves through the branches of the trees, it carries words meant only for you. There is a language in the wind, and you have become more familiar with that language, whether you know it or not. It is the wind that brought you to the lake. It is the wind that brought you to the Lady of the Mist."

Just then I heard a flapping sound. I looked up, and in the tree, settling its huge expanse of wings, was a giant peregrine falcon. It looked down at us, cocked its head, and screamed. Grandmother stood up and walked several yards away through a thicket of mulberry. On the other side she lifted up her arm. It was the first time I had noticed she had a band of leather wrapped around her wrist. She had her back turned to me. As she lifted up her arm, the falcon swooped down, wheeling to the left and then to the right. Then flapping his huge wings, he settled gently down onto her arm.

Slowly, Grandmother turned, her shawl falling away from her hair and down around her shoulders. Her hair was no longer white, but hung long and dark and curly down to her waist. She turned to me, and she was no longer the old woman but the woman I had seen at the lake, the Lady in the Mist. As she held the falcon up at shoulder height, her eyes flashed gold and green like the eyes of her bird of prey. She walked toward me.

"There is only one thing you must remember," she said, looking at me directly. Her voice sounded much younger and had a new melodious